A JOURNEY NORTH

Also by Louis P. Masur

The Sum of Our Dreams: A Concise History of America

Lincoln's Last Speech: Wartime Reconstruction and the Crisis of Reunion

Lincoln's Hundred Days: The Emancipation Proclamation and the War for the Union

The Civil War: A Concise History

Runaway Dream: Born to Run and Bruce Springsteen's American Vision

The Soiling of Old Glory: The Story of a Photograph that Shocked America

Autumn Glory: Baseball's First World Series)

1831: Year of Eclipse

Rites of Execution: Capital Punishment and the Transformation of American Culture, 1776–1865

A JOURNEY NORTH

JEFFERSON, MADISON, AND THE FORGING OF A FRIENDSHIP

LOUIS P. MASUR

OXFORD
UNIVERSITY PRESS

Oxford University Press is a department of the University of Oxford.
It furthers the University's objective of excellence in research, scholarship,
and education by publishing worldwide. Oxford is a registered trade mark of
Oxford University Press in the UK and certain other countries.

Published in the United States of America by Oxford University Press
198 Madison Avenue, New York, NY 10016, United States of America.

© Oxford University Press 2025

All rights reserved. No part of this publication may be reproduced, stored in a retrieval
system, transmitted, used for text and data mining, or used for training artificial
intelligence, in any form or by any means, for commercial purposes, without the
prior permission in writing of Oxford University Press, or as expressly permitted by law,
by license or under terms agreed with the appropriate reprographics rights organization.
Enquiries concerning reproduction outside the scope of the above should be sent to
the Rights Department, Oxford University Press, at the address above.

You must not circulate this work in any other form
and you must impose this same condition on any acquirer

Library of Congress Cataloging-in-Publication Data
Names: Masur, Louis P., author.
Title: A journey north : Jefferson, Madison, and the forging
of a friendship / Louis P. Masur.
Other titles: Jefferson, Madison, and the forging of a friendship
Description: New York, NY : Oxford University Press, 2025. |
Includes bibliographical references and index.
Identifiers: LCCN 2025001480 (print) | LCCN 2025001481 (ebook) |
ISBN 9780197684917 (hardback) | ISBN 9780197685051 | ISBN 9780197684931 (epub)
Subjects: LCSH: Jefferson, Thomas, 1743–1826—Friends and associates. |
Madison, James, 1751–1836—Friends and associates. |
Jefferson, Thomas, 1743–1826—Travel—New York (State) |
Madison, James, 1751–1836—Travel—New York (State) |
Hessian fly. | New York (State)—Description and travel.
Classification: LCC E332.2 .M367 2025 (print) | LCC E332.2 (ebook) |
DDC 973.4/110922—dc23/eng/20250224
LC record available at https://lccn.loc.gov/2025001480
LC ebook record available at https://lccn.loc.gov/2025001481

DOI: 10.1093/oso/9780197684917.001.0001

Printed by Sheridan Books, Inc., United States of America

For My Grandsons:
Evan Saul Jaffe
Ethan Frido Masur
Jason Herb Masur
Henry Seth Jaffe

Contents

List of Illustrations	ix
Preface	xi
Prologue: Travelers	1
Before the Journey	7
The Journey	
At Poughkeepsie: The Hessian Fly (May 23)	37
At Fort George: Prince Taylor (June 1)	57
At Bennington: Sugar Maple (June 4–5)	74
At Poospatuck: Unkechaug Indians (June 14)	95
Epilogue: Farewells	115
Acknowledgments	125
Notes	127
Further Reading	159
Index	161

Illustrations

Figure 1 *Jefferson to Madison, September 1, 1785, with a List of Books (Library of Congress)* 10

Figure 2 *Jefferson's Distance Traveled and Ratings of Inns, 1791 (Library of Congress)* 40

Figure 3 *Hessian Fly from A. S. Packard,* The Hessian Fly: Its Ravages, Habits, Enemies and Means of Preventing Its Increase *(Washington, DC: Government Printing Office, 1880)* 42

Figure 4 *Jefferson's Notes on the Hessian Fly, 1791 (Library of Congress)* 51

Figure 5 *Madison's Journal Entry on Prince Taylor, June 1, 1791 (private collection)* 65

Figure 6 *Sugar Maple Tree (Library of Congress)* 85

Figure 7 *Catalog of Prince Nursery, 1771 (Special Collections, Oregon State University)* 90

Figure 8 *Vocabulary of the Unquachog Indians (American Philosophical Society)* 105

Figure 9 *Blank Vocabulary List (American Philosophical Society)* 109

Figure 10 *Comparative Vocabularies of Several Indian Languages (American Philosophical Society)* 110

Figure 11 *Gilbert Stuart, "Portrait of Thomas Jefferson," ca. 1805–1807 (Bowdoin College Museum of Art)* 116

Figure 12 *Gilbert Stuart, "Portrait of James Madison," ca. 1805–1807 (Bowdoin College Museum of Art)* 117

Figure 13 *Jefferson's Walking Stick (Thomas Jefferson Foundation at Monticello)* 123

Preface

This is a short book about a brief journey taken in the late spring of 1791 by Thomas Jefferson and James Madison. They left only scant documentation: partial journals; field notes; a list of inns; words scrawled on an envelope; and some correspondence. But it is enough to trace the contours of the trip and what marked it: the Hessian fly, one of the greatest pests to crops of the day; an exchange with a free Black farmer, whom they met at Fort George; attention to the sugar maple tree; and notes on an encounter with several members of the Unkechaug, a tribe located on eastern Long Island. These topics, scattered as they might seem at first, reflect the breadth of these men's interests in entomology, racial classification, botany, and linguistics and their ideas about horticulture, history, and anthropology. The northern journey allows us to see Jefferson and Madison in a different light, not just as politicians, but as tourists and friends.

The journey, from May 21 to June 16, 1791, was taken at a precarious moment. Political parties had emerged that pitted Jefferson and Madison on one side and Alexander Hamilton and John Adams on the other, feuding over issues that would determine the future of the nation. The trip provided escape from the cauldron of political engagement and its toll on their spirits and physical well-being. A gambol through upstate New York and parts of New England offered them the promise of recovering both.

Of course, however much they may have desired to leave politics behind, politics always followed them, and their adversaries viewed the trip as politically motivated—an attempt to bolster Democratic-Republican support in a decidedly Federalist region. No doubt there was a political dimension to Jefferson and Madison's tours of Revolutionary battlefields, their conversations with local officials, and their visit to the new state of Vermont. Politics, however, was not their focus; an excursion, maybe an adventure, was.

Most of all, the trip was about their friendship. They had traveled together before, mainly between Philadelphia and Virginia. That was for political affairs. This was for curiosity and recreation, to go places they had never really been, and to do it together. It was a road trip to explore, learn, and escape. Nearly forty years later, Madison recalled that the northern journey made them "immediate companions."[1]

There is no friendship like theirs in American history, certainly not in political history. It thrived for fifty years. Fortunately, they exchanged more than 1,200 letters over that time, so we can trace their collaboration, both before the trip and after.[2]

In 1839, during an oration on the fiftieth anniversary of George Washington's inauguration, John Quincy Adams marveled at Jefferson and Madison: "The mutual influence of these two mighty minds upon each other is a phenomenon, like the invisible and mysterious movements of the magnet in the physical world, and in which the sagacity of the future historian may discover the solution of much of our national history not otherwise easily accountable."[3]

This book will not offer a solution to our national history by radically altering our view of its key founders. Its ambitions are more modest: to travel with Jefferson and Madison, to investigate what fascinated them, and to illuminate their incomparable friendship.

Prologue: Travelers

Thomas Jefferson loved to travel; James Madison, not so much. Jefferson crossed the ocean twice and, while in Europe, journeyed widely. His efforts nonetheless pale in comparison to those of Benjamin Franklin, who traversed the Atlantic eight times, toured Germany and France, explored Ireland and Scotland, and scrambled to Canada and distant points of western settlement. As a diplomat, John Adams crossed the Atlantic six times (on one of those trips, the ship nearly sank after sailing into a violent gale and springing a leak). George Washington left North America only once, when, in 1751, he sailed to Barbados, where he became infected with smallpox. What he did not explore abroad, he made up for in North America where, as president, over two tours, he visited every state of the nation and covered 1,700 miles. Alexander Hamilton only traveled once outside of North America, the journey from the West Indies that brought him in 1772. Madison largely limited his travels to trips between Virginia, Pennsylvania, New Jersey, and New York.

At age twenty, Jefferson asked his friend and classmate John Page, "Have you an inclination to travel, Page? Because if you have I shall be glad of your company." He said he intended to visit "particularly England Holland France Spain Italy (where I would buy me a good fiddle) and Egypt and return through the British provinces to the northward home." He hoped the journey would provide the added benefit of curing him of his feelings toward a woman (he would propose to Rebecca Burwell, who rejected his entreaties).[1]

It would be nearly twenty-five years before Jefferson satisfied part of his itinerary. Appointed minister plenipotentiary, he traveled to Europe in 1784. In 1786, he toured the English countryside with John Adams. He carried with him a copy of Thomas Whately's *Observations on Modern Gardening* and made inquiries "directed chiefly to such practical things as might enable me to estimate the expence of making and maintaining a garden in that style."[2]

The following year, he spent three months and covered 1,200 miles touring France and Italy. He traveled as a private citizen, not a diplomat, and brought no valets with him, instead hiring according to his needs in each town. "I was alone thro the whole," he boasted on his return, "and think one travels more usefully when they travel alone, because they reflect more." He kept an extensive journal of notes on his tour and reported that "Architecture, painting, sculpture, antiquities, agriculture, the condition of the labouring poor fill all my moments." He also sampled various wines and overall delighted in his journey. At Aix-en-Provence he wrote, "I am now in the land of corn, wine, oil, and sunshine. What more can man ask of heaven?"[3]

Finally, in 1788, Jefferson toured Holland and the Rhine Valley and again produced wide-ranging memoranda. He noted that Cologne "is the most northern spot on earth where wine is made," and he completed drawings of tables and wheelbarrows and gates. He also observed, "the transition from ease and opulence to extreme poverty is remarkable on crossing the line between the Dutch and Prussian territory." The soil was the same; the government different—the one a republic, the other a monarchy. But it was grapes and vineyards, not politics and policies that almost always absorbed Jefferson's attention.[4]

On his return, the seasoned traveler gave advice. In a letter written in June 1788, Jefferson offered "Hints to Americans Travelling in Europe," composed for Thomas Lee Shippen and John Rutledge, Jr., twenty-somethings about to embark on their version of the Grand Tour, a customary trip through Europe taken as a rite of passage for affluent young men. The advice ran to 5,000 words as Jefferson went city by city and made specific suggestions about such topics as roads, taverns (in Tains-l'hermitage, "do not go to the tavern at the Post house, the master of which is a most unconscionable rascal"), shops (in Strasbourg, the "bookseller here has the best shop of classical books I ever saw"), and the finest wines to drink. He also made general recommendations about "objects of attention for an American." In order, these consisted of Agriculture, Gardens, Architecture, Painting, Politics, and Courts. Finally, he offered this advice: "When you are doubting whether a thing is worth the trouble of going to

PROLOGUE

3

see, recollect that you will never again be so near it, that you may repent the not having seen it, but can never repent having seen it. But there is an opposite extreme too. That is, the seeing too much. A judicious selection is to be aimed at, taking care that the indolence of the moment have no influence on the decision."[5] As much as Jefferson relished travel, he recognized that it could create uneasiness, even misery. Jefferson wrote his seventeen-year-old nephew Peter Carr that traveling "makes men wiser, but less happy. When men of sober age travel, they gather knowledge which they may apply usefully for their country, but they are subject ever after to recollections mixed with regret, their affections are weakened by being extended over more objects, and they learn new habits which cannot be gratified when they return home." Jefferson confessed that his "observations are founded in experience." Perhaps all the European splendor felt corrupting. Perhaps the endless parade of glowing objects—paintings, castles, vast vineyards—made each succeeding object "insufficient to make themselves or anybody else happy." Do not travel to Europe in hopes of learning anything useful to your country, he advised. Instead, travel in the United States: "There is no place where your pursuit of knowledge will be so little obstructed by foreign objects as in your own country, nor any wherein the virtues of the heart will be less exposed to be weakened."[6]

If Europe was not for his teenage nephew, it might still be for his friend James Madison. In 1784, before his wide-ranging European travels, Jefferson invited Madison to spend the summer with him in France. He offered him food and lodging and calculated that the trip would cost no more than 200 guineas. For that price, "you will . . . have purchased the knowledge of another world."[7]

Madison responded several months later and offered multiple excuses for why he could not accept the invitation. (Madison was master of the omnibus excuse.) He said if he ever visited Europe, he would like to spend more time than just the summer. He said it would be inconvenient to travel at that moment because it would interrupt the work he was doing. Finally, the sickly Madison got to the crux of it: "I have some reason also to suspect that crossing the sea would be unfriendly to a singular disease of my constitution."[8]

It was not the last invitation to travel that he would turn down. In July 1785, James Monroe, a rising star in Virginia politics, wrote

Madison, "What say you to a trip to the Indian Treaty to be held on the Ohio—sometime in August or Sepr. I have thoughts of it & shod. be happy in your company." Monroe was referring to a treaty that would govern the frontier, and he intended an excursion to the area. Madison wrote a tortured response. He read the invitation, he said, and was inclined to accept, but then other considerations forced him to hesitate: the expense of such a trip concerned him; he might be called to public business and could not afford to spare so much time; there might be delays because who knows when the treaty would actually be signed (here, Madison had a point: the Treaty of Fort Finney was not signed until January 1786, and even Monroe returned from Ohio before it was completed). Finally, given the uncertainties of "travelling back thro' the Wilderness via Kentucky," it was impossible to calculate how long the journey would take.[9]

Monroe, in his original invitation, had also suggested treks to Montreal and Quebec or a ramble through the eastern states. These two offers Madison also rejected, the one because it would take too much time and might not be the best place for a U.S. citizen to visit and the second for all the reasons he had already given as well as wanting to travel only by land and not sea. Clearly, Madison was not ready to embark on any sort of journey.

Besides, he only just the year before, in 1784, traveled to Fort Schuyler, a hundred miles west of Albany. That trip was as much accident as intent. At Baltimore, he met with the Marquis de Lafayette, who was touring America and just visited with George Washington at Mt. Vernon. Lafayette had arrived in New York on August 4, and the returning hero of the American Revolution, who had served on Washington's staff and led troops at numerous battles, including Yorktown, was feted wherever he went. Madison informed Jefferson, "wherever he passes he receives the most flattering tokens of sincere affection from all ranks."[10]

Madison said Lafayette's plan was to travel to New York, Rhode Island, Boston, and then through Albany to Fort Schuyler. Madison told his father, "He presses me much to fall into his plan, and I am not sure that I shall decline it," and wrote Jefferson, "I have some thoughts of making this tour with him." In the end, Madison and Lafayette traveled to New York and then on September 15 took a barge up the Hudson to Albany and on to Fort Schuyler (named

PROLOGUE 5

Fort Stanwix before the Revolution). He had made the trip up the Hudson once before, in 1774 when he was twenty-three, apparently to "see the country." The trip in 1784 was not quite the "ramble into the Eastern States" that Madison was thinking about at the time because of the "need of exercise after a very sedentary period." It would suffice, however, and who, after all, could resist the opportunity to accompany Lafayette?[11]

Lafayette, Madison, and a small travel party that now included Francois Barbe-Mabois, the French charge d'affaires in America, left Albany on September 27. They stopped at the Shaker settlement at Niskayuna, founded in 1779, and witnessed the Shakers' religious contortions. They arrived on horseback at Fort Schuyler on September 29. The next day, they traversed muddy roads and dense forests and visited the Oneida nation, some 18 miles away. The treaty conference opened on October 3, and Lafayette addressed the assembled tribes. Madison told Jefferson that Lafayette was "recd. by the Indians with equal proofs of attachment as have been shewn him elsewhere in America." Madison praised Lafayette's "considerable talents," yet also noted "his strong thirst of praise and popularity." (Decades later, collecting his letters for publication, Madison would edit out his original assessment.) Madison and Lafayette departed before completion of the Treaty of Fort Stanwix, which was finalized on October 24. Under its terms, the Iroquois ceded their claims to tribal territory in western New York and the Ohio Valley. Madison thought the upshot of the treaty uncertain.[12]

Following his return to Albany from Fort Schuyler, Madison left Lafayette and traveled back to New York and Philadelphia. Overall, he described the trip as "extremely pleasing" and told Jefferson that it had "rather inflamed than extinguished my curiosity to see the Northern & N. W. Country," though he would never again travel that far into the frontier. Jefferson complimented his friend on his travels: "I find you thought it worth while to pass the last summer in exploring the woods of America, and I think you were right." Madison still had in mind a tour of the eastern states, and he told Jefferson in 1785 that "I must postpone the gratification, with a purpose of embracing it on the first convenient opportunity." That opportunity came in 1791. The northern journey would be the last major excursion either would take for the remainder of their lives.[13]

Before the Journey

On his way from Philadelphia to New York to meet Madison to embark on the trip, Jefferson stopped in Princeton to have his hair done. James Hemings, enslaved by Jefferson, accompanied him. In 1784, Abigail Adams commented on Jefferson's fussiness with his hair: "He expects not to live above a Dozen years and he shall lose one of those in hair dressing." In seven years, nothing had changed in that regard, and Jefferson made certain to look his best for his arrival in New York.[1]

Madison first mentioned the journey in March 1791, when he wrote his brother Ambrose that he was "not sure that I may not make a trip into New England" before returning to Virginia from Philadelphia. He thought it was a convenient time to travel, and he hoped "to form a party for the purpose." A month later he informed James Monroe that he "shall in company with Mr. Jefferson make a trip as far as Lake George," the site of Fort Ticonderoga. He even prepared a list of prospective taverns and lodgings in the Hudson Valley, noting whether they were good or bad. Madison and Jefferson exchanged letters over possible routes. Jefferson proposed that "when we tack about from the extremity of our journey, instead of coming back the same way, to cross over through Vermont to Connecticut river and down that to New-haven, then through Long-island to N.Y. and so to Philada." Madison had no objection. Excited about the upcoming trip, Madison exclaimed, "Health recreation & curiosity being my objects, I can never be out of my way."[2]

Health was a constant concern for both men. Jefferson explained to George Washington that he was embarking on a trip with Madison in part to "get rid of a headache which is very troublesome, by giving more exercise to the body & less to the mind." All winter and spring through 1791 he suffered from an "almost constant headach."

Jefferson's correspondence is peppered with references to "a violent head ach" (1764), "an inveterate head ach" (1776), an "attack of my periodical headach" (1784). In May 1790, he described his headache as "violent" and in June "very violent." In 1807, he was "obliged to be shut up in a dark room from early in the forenoon till night, with a periodical head-ache."[3]

James Madison, too, was not well. His cousin wrote him in April 1791 and expressed "real Concern" that Madison's political activities "has been the means of impairing your health." Madison's health, it seems, was always impaired. Short and slight and weighing approximately 100 pounds, Madison lamented his "very infirm health" and the "discouraging feebleness of his Constitution."[4]

Throughout his life, Madison suffered attacks that he thought resembled epilepsy and "suspended all intellectual function." His seizures, whatever their cause (and acute anxiety attacks brought on by stress cannot be discounted), made him hypervigilant about his delicate health, which no doubt contributed to his frailty. In 1772, only twenty-one years old, he wrote, "I am too dull and infirm now to look out for any extraordinary things in this world for I think my sensations for many months past have intimated to me not to expect a long or healthy life."[5]

Across their half-century friendship, Jefferson and Madison often commented to one another about their health. For example, in 1784, Jefferson told Madison that he suffered from a "double-quotidian head-ache"; in 1801, Madison complained, "my health still suffers." Illness was a frequent refrain.

They first met in 1776, when they participated in the Virginia General Assembly in Williamsburg. Jefferson was 6'2" and Madison 5'4" and the shorter man no doubt looked up to the taller in more than height. Jefferson was eight years older and had, of course, authored the Declaration of Independence. In fall 1776, they served together on several committees, notably the Committee on Religion, where they worked toward disestablishment from the Anglican Church and the advancement of the free exercise of religion. In 1779, Madison served with Jefferson on the Executive Council. As both later recalled, that was when they became friends. Madison noted that "an intimacy took place" when they worked together, and Jefferson recalled that he had known Madison "intimately . . . from 1779."[6]

BEFORE THE JOURNEY 9

When not dealing with military matters, finance, trade, and Indian relations, among other topics, they bonded over books. The first mention of Madison by Jefferson is from November 29, 1776, when he recorded that he received money from Madison for books. "I cannot live without books," Jefferson once wrote, and Madison no doubt felt the same. Together in Philadelphia in January 1783, Jefferson contributed titles to the list of books Madison was compiling for creation of a library for the Confederation Congress (a resolution to purchase the volumes was defeated). Across decades of friendship, they pored over catalogues, compiled lists of titles, visited booksellers, and sent one another books and pamphlets, sometimes by the crate: Jefferson once included 207 volumes in a single shipment. "In the purchase of books, pamphlets &c. old & curious, or new & useful, I shall ever keep you in my eye," Jefferson wrote Madison in 1784. After Jefferson's death in 1826, Madison referred to him as a "walking library."[7]

Though on close terms only for a brief period, Madison played a key role in coaxing Jefferson back into public life after he left the governorship under a cloud in 1781. With British troops coursing through Virginia, Jefferson seemed powerless to counter their thrust, and Virginians blamed him for the chaos. In June 1781, he was nearly captured by British forces and, with his term nearing its end, he retired to his estate at Poplar Forest. The General Assembly launched an investigation into Jefferson's conduct as governor; in December, they acquitted him of any accusations of cowardice or malfeasance. No matter. The investigation wounded him deeply, and he retreated. For months, he limited his political correspondence. In May 1782, he told James Monroe that he intended to retire from public life and instead embrace "my farm, my family and books from which I think nothing will ever separate me." The charges that had been made against him, he declared, "inflicted a wound on my spirit that will only be cured by the all-healing grave."[8]

Privately, Madison was unsympathetic to Jefferson's peevish behavior. He told Edmund Randolph, Virginia's attorney general, that "the mode in which he seems determined to revenge the wrong received from his Country does not appear to me to be dictated either by philosophy or patriotism." Madison tried to assuage Jefferson, telling him that the investigation had made little impression on him.[9]

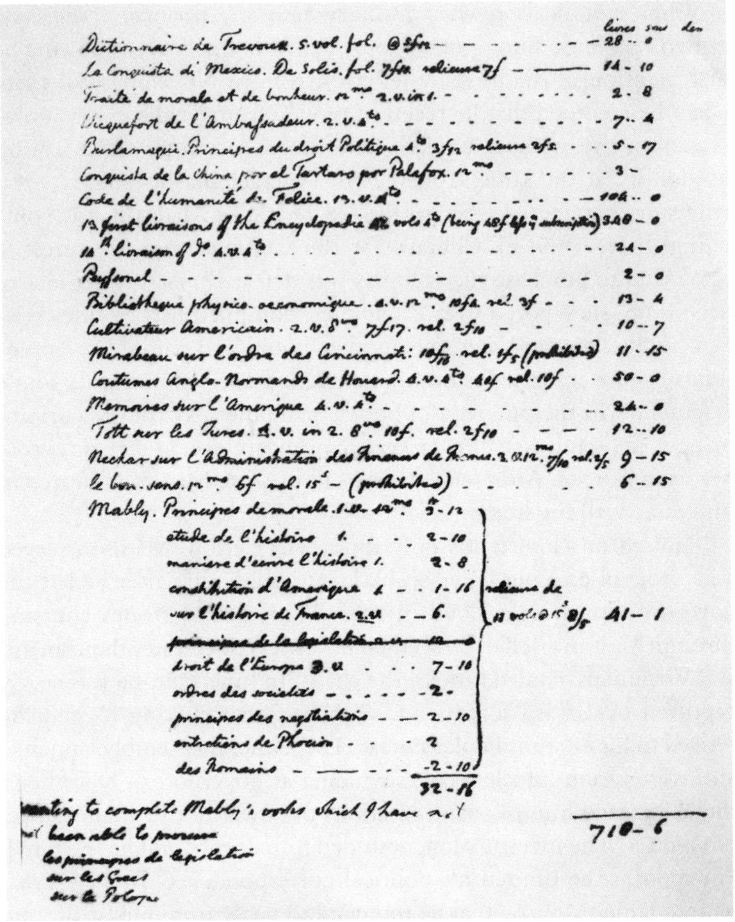

livres sous den
Dictionnaire de Trevoux. 5. vol. fol. @ 5₶ - - - - - - - - - 28 .. 0
La Conquista di Mexico. De Solis. fol. 7₶ reliure 7f - —— 14 - 10
Traité de morale et de bonheur. 12mo. 2. v. in 1. - - - - - - - 2 . 8
Wicquefort de l'Ambassadeur. 2. v. 4to. - - - - - - - - - - 7 .. 4
Burlamaqui. Principes du droit Politique 4to. 3₶ reliure 2f. - - - 5 - 17
Conquista de la China por el Tartaro por Palafox. 12mo. - - - - - - 3 -
Code de l'humanité de Felice. 13. v. 4to. - - - - - - - - 104 .. 0
13 first livraisons of the Encyclopedie [illegible] vols 4to (being [illegible] subscription) 340 - 0
14th. livraison of do. 4. v. 4to. . . . . 24 - 0
Buffonel - - - - - - - - - - - - - - 2 - 0
Bibliotheque physico-oeconomique. 4. v. 12mo. 10f4. rel. 3f - - - 13 - 4
Cultivateur Americain. 2. v. 8vo. 7f17. rel. 2f10 - - - 10 -- 7
Mirabeau sur l'ordre des Cincinnati: 10f10 rel. 1f5 (prohibited) 11 . 15
Coutumes Anglo-Normands de Houard. 4. v. 4to. 40f rel. 10f . . 50 - 0
Memoires sur l'Amerique 4. v. 4to. - - - - - - - - - 24 .. 0
Tott sur les Turcs. 4. v. in 2. 8vo. 10f. rel. 2f10 - - - - 12 .. 10
Neckar sur l'Administration des Finances de France. 3. v. 12mo. 7/10 rel. 2/5 9 - 15
le bon-sens. 12mo. 6f rel. 15s - (prohibited) - - - - - 6 - 15
Mably. Principes de morale. 1. v. 12mo. 2 - 12
étude de l'histoire 1. - - - 2 - 10
maniere d'ecrire l'histoire 1. 2 - 8
constitution d'Amerique 1 - - - 1 - 16
sur l'histoire de France. 2. v. - - 6.
~~principes de la legislation [illegible]~~
droit de l'Europe 3. v. . . . . 7 - 10
ordres des societés - - - - - - - 2 -
principes des negociations - — 2 - 10
entretiens de Phocion - - - 2
des Romains - —— - - - 2 - 10
32 - 16
reliure de 11 vols @ 15s 8/5 41 - 1
wanting to complete Mably's works which I have not been able to procure
les principes de legislation
sur les Grecs
sur la Pologne
718 - 6

Figure 1 Jefferson to Madison, September 1, 1785, with a List of Books (Library of Congress)

Tragedy changed Jefferson's trajectory. In September 1782, Jefferson's wife, Martha Wayles Skelton, died after giving birth in May. It was her sixth child, only two of whom would live to adulthood. Jefferson was inconsolable. In November he wrote, "a single event wiped away all my plans and left me a blank which I had not the spirits to fill up." Madison thought the tragedy might induce

BEFORE THE JOURNEY 11

Jefferson to return to public life, and he was right. In August 1781, Jefferson had declined an appointment as minister plenipotentiary to negotiate peace. In the aftermath of Martha Jefferson's death, Madison moved that Congress renew the appointment. It was agreed to unanimously. Jefferson accepted and he arrived in Philadelphia at the end of December to ready for the transatlantic journey. He and Madison had not seen one another for three years.[10]

Together in Philadelphia, their friendship deepened. They stayed at Mary House's lodgings, located at Fifth and Market. Jefferson would reside at the boardinghouse on future visits, at one point asking Madison about lodging and emphasizing that "a room to myself, if it be but a barrack, is indispensable." Madison would again room there in the summer of 1787 during the Constitutional Convention. Jefferson witnessed and encouraged Madison's romantic pursuit of fifteen-year-old Catherine "Kitty" Floyd, daughter of William Floyd, a signer of the Declaration of Independence. The courtship ended when she called off a potential engagement.[11]

Politics proved less fickle. Madison and Jefferson adopted a cipher to use in their correspondence to keep delicate matters secret from the eyes of prying postmasters. It was a book code based on Thomas Nugent's *New Pocket Dictionary of the French and English Languages* (1774). Several weeks before Jefferson arrived in Philadelphia, Madison complained to Edmund Randolph that "the want of a cypher" with Jefferson kept him from communicating confidential information. The writer would encode the word by the column and line where it appeared in a certain book. They used the second edition of Nugent's dictionary and paginated the numbers themselves. Jefferson first used it in a letter to Madison from Baltimore, where he awaited passage to Paris. Madison employed code in his return letter on February 11, 1783, to gossip about John Adams, noting his "display of his vanity, his prejudice against the French Court and his venom against Doctr. Franklin." Several years later, Jefferson would write in code that Adams was "vain" and "irritable," but that he was amiable and thought Madison would "love him if ever you become acquainted with him." That opinion shifted with the political warfare of the 1790s.[12]

The two men would change the code they used. In 1785, Jefferson told Madison that he had "made a cypher on a more convenient plan than the one we have used." They employed it thereafter, though over time each used a variety of codes. The only occasion on which a cipher would prove unnecessary was when they were together, but there would be no in-person contact while Jefferson served in France from 1784 to 1789.[13]

Before Jefferson departed, he and Madison spent a month in Philadelphia from October to November 1783. In addition to discussions of politics and diplomacy, they visited bookstores and pursued scientific interests (Jefferson bought a thermometer; weather obsessed him). He also nominated his friend for election to the American Philosophical Society, which Benjamin Franklin among others had founded in 1743, and which, after a lull, became fully operational in 1769. Following their time together, Jefferson wrote his nephew, who was studying near Madison's home in Montpelier, that Madison's "judgment is so sound and his heart so good that I wish you to respect every advice he would be so kind to give you, equally as if it came from me."[14]

We are fortunate that distance compelled them to correspond. Their letters through the 1780s chart their growing personal friendship and political partnership. After Madison's broken engagement to Kitty Floyd, Jefferson offered philosophical consolation. He told him to look forward and assured his friend that "the world still presents the same and many other resources of happiness, and you possess many within yourself."[15]

In 1784, Jefferson implored Madison to buy property near him in Monticello. He told him that James Monroe was purchasing land near Monticello, and that William Short (his future private secretary) was considering it as well. "What I would not give [if] you could fall into the circle," he wrote. What he called "rational society," a coterie of nearby friends, "informs the mind, sweetens the temper, cheers our spirits, and promotes health."[16]

Part of that time together was spent playing chess. Jefferson loved the game, which he once referred to as "a matter of science." He purchased numerous chess sets and chess books. His granddaughter recalled that he was "a very good chess-player," and that he and Madison often played games that lasted four hours. Madison owned *The Elements of Chess: A Treatise Combining Theory with Practice* (1805), and one correspondent complimented him on his passion for the game. In 1801, Jefferson wrote Madison that he was looking forward to seeing at Monticello "mrs Madison [Madison married in 1794],

BEFORE THE JOURNEY

yourself & the Chess heroine," a reference to Anna Payne, Dolley Madison's younger sister and a devoted player, who undoubtedly earned her nickname by triumphing over Jefferson on the chess board.[17]

To get him to move closer, Jefferson appointed himself Madison's real estate agent, notifying him of a little farm of 140 acres adjacent to his land that was for sale. Madison responded that he was moved by Jefferson's "affectionate invitation," but said he could not yet embrace the idea. Perhaps one day. Jefferson did not give up. A year later, he asked Monroe if he had done anything about moving near Monticello. "I keep my eye on yourself and Short for society and do not despair of Madison."[18]

Through the 1780s, they wrote about every matter of public policy: finance, trade, foreign affairs, military reorganization, western territories, and constitutions. In 1784, Madison asked Jefferson to buy him books on "whatever may throw light on the general Constitution and droit public [public law] of the several confederacies which have existed." With discussion in the air of ways for strengthening the "band of Union," Jefferson once advised Madison to keep any specific proposals confidential until fully explained as "I have found prejudices frequently produced against propositions handed to the world without explanation or support."[19]

No correspondence between them was more pointed than their exchanges between 1787 and 1789 over the newly proposed Constitution, which emerged from the convention held in Philadelphia from May 25 to September 17, 1787, and at which Madison, of course, played a central role. "The evidence of dangerous defects in the Confederation," Madison wrote Jefferson in December 1786, had led to the call for a Constitutional Convention in Philadelphia. When Jefferson replied on December 16, he apologized for his "very long silence" up to then. He explained that he had fractured his wrist and could hardly write, except with his left hand. The fracture had occurred in September on a stroll with Maria Cosway, a married Italian-English artist with whom Jefferson became smitten. He confessed none of the details to Madison, nor to anyone else for that matter.[20]

In their letters, they differed over their reaction to Shays's Rebellion, an armed uprising in western Massachusetts against taxes and indebtedness and a state government located in Boston that seemed indifferent to the problems of farmers. Creditors in the east offered no relief to debtors in the western part of the state. Northampton was the site of a protest in August 1786 that shut down the county court. The following year, a militia force fired on protesters as they approached the armory in Springfield. The rebellion had been broken, but the actions terrified elites who thought the Articles of Confederation were not equal to the task of providing a frame of government by which the nation would survive. Madison felt that the spirit of insurrection had to be subdued and that it threatened "the tranquility of the Union." He told Jefferson that he supported the use of the "vigorous measures" the state had employed to quell the unrest.[21]

Jefferson disagreed and offered Madison his thoughts on "the late troubles." Writing from Paris in January 1787, Jefferson explained that societies existed in three different ways: without government, "as among our Indians"; under a government "where every one has a just influence," as in the United States; or under a government of force, as in all monarchies. The first condition, no government, might be the best, but it was inconsistent with a large population. The third condition, monarchy, was the reign of "wolves over sheep." Only the second state allows "a precious degree of liberty and happiness" for everyone. The problem was the inherent evil of being susceptible to turbulence, which he thought served an important role nourishing attention to public affairs and checking "the degeneracy of government." He notably concluded that "a little rebellion now and then is a good thing, and as necessary in the political world as storms in the physical."[22]

By year's end, he had a copy of the newly drafted Constitution, courtesy of Madison. He had learned little about the Convention while it was taking place as the delegates had been sworn to secrecy, a decision that Jefferson felt set an "abominable" precedent. Madison promised to make amends to Jefferson for his required silence, assuring him that "if I ever have the pleasure of seeing you [I] shall be able to give you pretty full gratification."[23]

The document caused Jefferson concern. He confessed to John Adams that there were "things in it which stagger all my dispositions." He told William Stephens Smith, John Adams's son-in-law and a diplomat serving in London, that he thought there were good articles and bad, and was especially perturbed about the creation of

BEFORE THE JOURNEY

a chief executive, which he compared to "setting up a kite [bird of prey] to keep the hen yard in order." He believed that convention delegates were overreacting to the rebellion in Massachusetts. The occasional revolt (and Jefferson did the math: one rebellion in thirteen states independent for eleven years meant one rebellion every century and a half for each state) was welcome. "The tree of liberty," he famously argued, "must be refreshed from time to time with the blood of patriots and tyrants. It is its natural manure."[24]

In letters to Madison, Jefferson also expressed his apprehension that the proposed Constitution did not contain a bill of rights. Most Federalists thought it unnecessary. Hamilton, in Federalist 84, argued against one. He even suggested it might be dangerous to include one because it would suggest exceptions to powers that are not included in the Constitution and might therefore give reason to expand executive authority. Anti-Federalists, however, were mostly united in demanding a bill of rights, and, in Massachusetts, only an agreement by Federalists to support amendments to the Constitution assured ratification.[25]

Jefferson wrote in December 1787 that he did not like "the omission from the Constitution of a bill of rights, providing clearly & without the aid of sophisms for freedom of religion, freedom of the press, protection against standing armies, restriction against monopolies, the eternal & unremitting force of the habeas corpus laws, and trials by jury in all matters of fact triable by the laws of the land & not by the law of Nations." Madison replied that he favored a bill of rights, as long as it did not imply powers not intended. Still, he did not think its omission "a material defect" and confessed that he wasn't keen to include one simply because others wanted it. In the end, he supported it because "The political truths declared in that solemn manner acquire by degrees the character of fundamental maxims of free Government, and as they become incorporated with the national sentiment, counteract the impulses of interest and passion." Jefferson responded that he also thought a bill of rights would provide a check on the judiciary. As for the argument made by some that it was impossible to identify which rights to include, Jefferson wrote, "Half a loaf is better than no bread. If we cannot secure all our rights, let us secure what we can."[26]

On June 8, 1789, Madison introduced a proposed Bill of Rights to Congress. He offered a series of nineteen amendments, twelve of which Congress approved and sent to the states for ratification. The process was underway at the time of their northern journey in 1791, with seven states of the required eleven (two-thirds) ratifying ten of the proposed amendments. Vermont, the newest state, ratified on November 3, 1791, and became the tenth state to do so. A month later, on December 15, 1791, Virginia ratified, and the first ten amendments to the Constitution became law. Massachusetts did not ratify the original amendments until 1939, the sesquicentennial of the Bill of Rights. It was joined by Georgia and Connecticut.

Jefferson returned from Paris in November 1789, a month after Washington transmitted the twelve amendments to the states, and in March 1790 assumed the duties of secretary of state in Washington's administration. He and Madison, serving in the House of Representatives, were reunited, first at Monticello after Christmas ("I had the happiness of possessing you at Monticello," Jefferson wrote in January) and then in New York, when Jefferson arrived on March 21. A few days earlier, in Philadelphia, he exulted to Benjamin Rush that Madison "was the greatest man in the world."[27]

On June 20, 1790, Jefferson hosted a dinner with Madison and Hamilton that led to an agreement that would create a national capital along the Potomac River. They met at 57 Maiden Lane, his New York residence. Jefferson lived in the house from May until September and rented it for 100 pounds a year. He hosted many gatherings there, but none more important than the meeting with Hamilton and Madison, intended to resolve what Jefferson saw as the two central issues before Congress. On that day, emerging from a headache that "kept me long in a lingering state," he wrote to Monroe, "Congress has been long embarrassed by two of the most irritating questions that ever can be raised among them, 1. the funding the public debt, and 2. the fixing on a more central residence." He added, "Endeavours are therefore using to bring about a disposition to some mutual sacrifices." "Mutual sacrifice of opinion and interest is become the duty of every one," he told his son-in-law that same day.[28]

Hamilton had addressed the issue of the public debt in his *Report on Public Credit*, submitted to Congress in January. Seeking to solve the problem of a national debt that crippled the nation's credit, Hamilton proposed that Congress fund the debt, which stood at nearly 80 million dollars. The United States government would consolidate the residual debt from the Revolutionary War and make regular payments of principal and interest on any outstanding certificates. Moreover, these certificates would be funded at par—full value—even though many bondholders had sold them for pennies on the dollar to reap what they could. Revenue from tariffs and other government sources of income would be set aside to provide the necessary resources to fund the debt, which meant paying interest on it rather than paying it off. In this way, the United States would send a strong signal to creditors that the newly created national government, established from the newly ratified Constitution, would honor its obligations while at the same time becoming a more powerful, energetic, centralized power.

Madison and Jefferson were among the opponents of a funded debt. The creation of a permanent debt seemed anathema to principles of good government. Madison called it "a public curse." Jefferson never lost his distaste for it. In 1817 he wrote, "I sincerely believe . . . that the principle of spending money to be paid by posterity, under the name of funding, is but swindling futurity on a large scale." Madison also condemned the failure to discriminate between original bondholders and speculators. He sought "equitable interference" so that the original bondholders also profited from any plan to fund the debt. His proposal, however, was rejected by Congress, most of whose members thought it impracticable to trace down original bondholders and insisted that private contracts could not be violated—doing so would set a precedent that would destroy the nation's credit.[29]

Funding and redemption were one matter; assumption another. Hamilton argued that the national government should assume some 25 million dollars of state debt. This would offer the advantage of creditors not having to deal with the vagaries of state-by-state policies and would further enhance the authority of the national government. Hamilton believed that this would lead to an "orderly, stable, and satisfactory arrangement of the national finances." It was a "measure of sound policy and substantial justice."[30]

The problem, in addition to enhancing the power of the national government, was that Hamilton's plan would consolidate the debt among the states. Not all states, however, were equally indebted—Virginia, for example, had largely paid off its obligations. Furthermore, before there could be assumption, there would need to be an accounting of what proportion of costs were held by each state to prosecute the war. Madison rejected the argument that states accrued their debts in the common cause of liberty and therefore they were in effect national debts. "The debts of the particular states cannot in any point of view be considered as actual debts of the United States," he insisted. Madison thought implementation of assumption, even if passed, impracticable, even unconstitutional. And he bristled at the suggestion of a Massachusetts delegate that failure to pass assumption would "endanger the union itself."[31]

Still, those "prophetic menaces" alarmed him, and, although opposed to assumption, Madison's tone softened and he urged that, whatever was decided, "patriotism and every other noble and generous motive" will lead the minority to acquiesce in measures decided to establish public credit. Of course, that was easy to say when you believed your view would prevail.[32]

In April, the House rejected Hamilton's funding proposal. It failed again in June. On the 20th, Jefferson held the private dinner that brought together Hamilton and Madison. Jefferson certainly understood the necessity of some version of Hamilton's plan to "save us from the greatest of all calamities, the total extinction of our credit in Europe," and he sought changes in the assumption plan "to divest it of its injustice." He relished playing the role of mediator.[33]

The only accounts of this famous dinner come from Jefferson, written at least two years after. He said he had been on his way to Washington's house when he had run into Hamilton whose "look was somber, haggard, and dejected beyond description." Appearing "uncouth and neglected," he approached Jefferson to discuss the nettlesome issue of assumption. Jefferson responded that having only recently arrived from France, he was not fully versed in domestic affairs. Nonetheless, he admitted that assumption struck him unfavorably, and he was concerned with the "mutual distrust and antipathy" between Northern and Southern representatives.[34]

"Persuaded that men of sound heads and honest views needed nothing more than explanation and mutual understanding to enable them to unite in some measures which might enable us to get along," Jefferson decided to bring together Hamilton and Madison. He said he played an "exhortatory" role in the discussion. A week after the dinner, Jefferson wrote to David Ramsay: "Funding plans are embarrassed with a proposition to assume the state debts, which is

BEFORE THE JOURNEY 19

as disagreeable to a part of the Union as desirable to another part. I hope some compromise will be found."[35]

In the end, Madison agreed to allow assumption to come again before Congress, though he maintained he would not vote for it. In return, since assumption of state debts would be "a bitter one to the Southern states, something should be done to soothe them." That something was an agreement to move the seat of government to the Potomac. Madison had told Washington two years earlier that he thought the seat of government needed to be closer to the interests of the burgeoning western territories and, under any circumstances, thought New York "extremely objectionable." He also thought Philadelphia should be shunned. To get the Residence Act through, the Pennsylvania delegation had to be persuaded, and Hamilton personally took on the task and convinced them to go along. Jefferson noted, "This is the real history of the assumption, about which many erroneous conjectures have been published. It was unjust, in itself oppressive to the states, and was acquiesced in merely from a fear of disunion, while our government was still in its most infant state." By the time Jefferson wrote this account, perhaps 1792, his animosity toward Hamilton knew no bounds, and he noted that the fiscal plan "enabled Hamilton so to strengthen himself by corrupt services to many." Later, he would write, "Hamilton was not only a monarchist, but a monarchy bottomed on corruption."[36]

The Residence Act and the Funding Act, both passed in the summer of 1790, formalized the compromise. The federal government assumed the state debts (terms were revised to be more favorable to Virginia), and the capital would relocate to Philadelphia for ten years while a permanent site on the Potomac was created.

What Jefferson did not say in his recollection was that James Hemings prepared the meal on which the three men dined—capon stuffed with truffles, Virginia ham, boeuf à la mode, a selection of macaroons and meringues, and for dessert a warm pastry puff filled with vanilla ice cream. Hemings had been brought to Monticello as a child, part of the estate of trader John Wayles, Jefferson's father-in-law, who died in 1773. Wayles had fathered James, as well as five other children, making him a half-brother to Jefferson's wife, Martha. James's mother, Elizabeth Hemings, headed an enslaved family that was the largest at Monticello. He served as Jefferson's personal servant while governor of Virginia during the war and was

20 A JOURNEY NORTH

trusted with care of his family. Appointed as a minister plenipotentiary to the French Court in 1784, Jefferson decided to bring nineteen-year-old James with him to Paris.

In a process that took three years, Jefferson had James trained in the art of French cooking, through apprenticeships with various chefs, including one at the renowned Château de Chantilly. Jefferson made James head chef at Hôtel de Langeac, the townhouse where Jefferson lived and conducted official business. Hemings oversaw a French staff and prepared the meals for the countless dinner parties Jefferson hosted. He was paid 24 livres a month as chef de cuisine; it is unknown what he did with his wages. In France, he could have petitioned for his freedom.

Jefferson was fully aware of this possibility. In 1786, he advised Paul Bentalou, a former captain in the Continental Army, who wrote asking for advice on how his wife could get permission from the French ministry "to keep her Little Negro-Boy, while she Remains in the Kingdom." Jefferson responded, "I have known an instance where a person bringing in a slave, and saying nothing about it, has not been disturbed in his possession." That person was Jefferson. The minister said that "the laws of France give him freedom if he claims it, and that it will be difficult, if not impossible, to interrupt the course of the law." He advised that the less said the better and offered to seek a dispensation if Bentalou still desired one.[37]

Hemings never claimed his freedom and returned with Jefferson to the United States in 1789. He brought with him recipes that transformed American culinary tastes and included macaroni and cheese, fried potatoes, and crème brûlée. And in 1790, living with Jefferson in Philadelphia, Hemings again did not press for freedom, though he could have. The Gradual Abolition Act passed in 1780 provided that any enslaved person who moved to Pennsylvania would be freed after six months. Washington skirted the law by having his property sent out of state, if only for a day, to reset the clock. Jefferson did not engage in such maneuvers, yet James never sought his freedom.

Only in 1793 did Hemings pursue his freedom and Jefferson set the conditions:

> Having been at great expence in having James Hemings taught the art of cookery, desiring to befriend him, and to require from him as little in return as possible, I do hereby promise and declare,

BEFORE THE JOURNEY

that if the said James shall go with me to Monticello in the course of the ensuing winter, when I go to reside there myself, and shall there continue until he shall have taught such person as I shall place under him for that purpose to be a good cook, this previous condition being performed, he shall be thereupon made free, and I will thereupon execute all proper instruments to make him free.[38]

Jefferson's words sting: His expense? Wanting to befriend him? Requiring little in return? Hemings agreed, and Jefferson chose James's brother Peter as replacement chef. Two years later, on February 5, 1796, James was freed, discharged "of all duties and claims of servitude."[39]

Once freed, James traveled and eventually settled in Baltimore. Elected president in 1800, Jefferson sought to hire Hemings as White House chef. In response to his inquiries, the president-elect heard from one former employee, who wrote that he had spoken to James: "according to your Desire he has made mention again as he did before that he was willing to serve you before any other man in the Union but sence he understands that he would have to be among strange servants he would be very much obliged to you if you would send him a few lines of engagement and on what conditions and what wages you would please to give him with your own hand wreiting." Jefferson, however, did not write James. He may have granted him his freedom, but he chose not to communicate with him directly. Sometime in the summer of 1801, Hemings returned to Monticello for a few weeks, and a few months later, back in Baltimore, committed suicide.[40]

Having helped broker the deal that stabilized the nation's credit in return for relocating the government, Jefferson searched for a residence in Philadelphia, where Congress would gather on December 6, 1790. He knew the city well, having first visited in 1766 to be inoculated against smallpox. He lived there from May to September 1776 and drafted the Declaration of Independence in his furnished rental at 7th and High Street (now Market). Jefferson sought a property that would likely be his residence for several years.

He was meticulous and demanding in his requests. Writing to William Temple Franklin, Benjamin's grandson, he explained his intention to take two houses and use the lower floors for public offices and first floors for private use. A third floor might hold "dead office papers." Franklin proposed several houses, and Jefferson preferred one owned by Thomas Leiper, a prominent tobacco merchant. Jefferson said "the part of town . . . and the landlord" led to his decision. He then explained that because of the price he would have to confine himself to one, not two, tenements and therefore required various changes, including a room over the kitchen and additional modifications in dividing the space. He also needed a stable for five horses and a carriage house. Jefferson added a book gallery and a garden. The pace of the construction frustrated him, and he complained to his daughter that "the workmen are so slow in finishing the house I rented here, I know not when I shall have it ready." He ended up paying more than the 80 pounds a year he desired (rent was 250 pounds) yet establishing a friendship with his landlord that lasted until Leiper's death in 1825.[41]

When Jefferson arrived in Philadelphia on November 21, 1790, his residence at 274 High Street was still not ready for occupation, and it would not be for several more weeks. He again resided at Mrs. House's, along with Madison, with whom he had spent substantial time since they had departed New York together on September 1 and traveled to Virginia. During that journey south, waiting to take a ferry across Chesapeake Bay to Annapolis, they ran into Thomas Lee Shippen, to whom, a few years earlier, Jefferson had given advice on traveling in Europe. Shippen wrote his father, "I never knew two men more agreeable than they were."[42]

During that trip home, Jefferson and Madison had visited Washington at Mt. Vernon and, on September 18, arrived at Madison's estate, what would come to be called Montpelier. Jefferson had never been there. He stayed overnight and the next day left for Monticello (less than 30 miles away) on a horse he borrowed from Madison and later purchased. The two bickered over the price, each desiring to be generous to the other. Jefferson did not want Madison to set the price because he consistently undervalued the cost of goods when it came to Jefferson. "I know nobody with whom it is so difficult to settle a price. . . . Witness the money disputes on our journey," admonished Jefferson. And then, before a price was established, the horse died. Madison argued that the death was evidence that the horse was not sound, and he wanted to absorb some of the cost. Jefferson refused, saying Madison bore no responsibility. Jefferson decided to overpay his bill to Madison for various expenses incurred on their trip; Madison refunded the money.[43]

The episode might have sundered their friendship. Instead, if anything, it brought them even closer together, outdoing one another in thoughtfulness and generosity. Madison had visited Jefferson in October, and the two of them traveled back to Philadelphia in November 1790. In March 1791, finally settled in his new home, he invited Madison to live with him. In a note, he asked, "what say you to taking a wade into the country at noon," and then implored him to consider whether he would "come and take a bed and plate with me." Jefferson thought the company at Mrs. House's might deteriorate with the arrival of George Beckwith, a British official and confidante of Alexander Hamilton. He explained he had plenty of space and could make a room available to him within twenty-four hours. Having him would provide "relief from a solitude of which I have too much," and he assured Madison that having him would not increase his expenses "an atom."[44]

Madison accepted the offer to take a walk and declined the invitation to relocate. Again, he provided a multicausal explanation for why he could not do something: he was just getting settled; his papers and books were all over the place; he was in harness working on a project; it would look too "pointed" were he to leave Mrs. House's just as a new resident arrived. Though he would not live with Jefferson, he would make amends, he said, by seeing him and dining with him as often as possible.[45]

Jefferson would soon be caught up in a political brouhaha that erupted while planning his northern journey with Madison. On April 26, 1791, he forwarded to a publisher a copy of Thomas Paine's *Rights of Man*, published in London earlier in the year. Madison had lent him the copy that he had received from John Beckley, a political ally and clerk of the House of Representatives (he would serve as the first librarian of Congress). Beckley was keen to see the pamphlet published in America and, unable to retrieve it himself, urged Jefferson to send it to the publisher. He duly forwarded it to Jonathan Bayard Smith, a prominent merchant, whom he mistakenly thought was the brother, rather than the father, of Samuel Harrison Smith, who would soon publish the first American edition of *Rights of Man*. A week after Jefferson forwarded the copy, the book was in print.

Jefferson received his copies and, as he later said, was "thunderstruck" to discover that a portion of the comment he made in his note to Samuel Smith was being included as part of the publisher's preface to promote the book. In his forwarding note, Jefferson had written in the third person, "he is extremely pleased to find it will be re-printed here, and that something at length to be publicly said against the political heresies which have sprung up among us. He has no doubt our citizens will rally a second time around the standard of Common sense." Smith did not say it was Beckley, not Jefferson, who wanted it forwarded for publication and identified Jefferson only as "Secretary of State," thus lending official sanction to the publication.[46]

Rights of Man was Paine's response to Edmund Burke's *Reflections on the Revolution in France*, published in November 1790. Burke, an Irishman and member of Parliament, denounced the French Revolution and, in doing so, became an avatar of conservatism. Writing between the storming of the Bastille and the start of the Reign of Terror, Burke foresaw the violence ahead. He defended established institutions, such as the church and the monarchy, and denounced revolutionary thinkers for their willingness to disregard experience. Against their declaration of "the rights of men," he observed, "there can be no prescription, against these no agreement is binding; these admit no temperament and no compromise."[47]

Paine denounced Burke's pamphlet as "an outrageous abuse on the French Revolution, and the principles of Liberty." He condemned Burke's adherence to ancient institutions and norms. "I am contending for the rights of the living," he declared, "and against their being willed away, and controuled and contracted for, by the . . . authority of the dead." Government was for the living, not the dead, and it is the living who must decide on what government is best for them. The French people, Paine noted, revolted against the despotism of the monarchy as an institution, not necessarily Louis XVI as the king. In France "we see a revolution generated in the rational contemplation of the rights of man, and distinguishing from the beginning between persons and principles." Those principles had guided the American Revolution and would now steer the French Revolution. Paine dedicated the work to George Washington.[48]

In praising Paine's work, Jefferson was reasserting his hatred of monarchy and nobility against those in America who seemed still

BEFORE THE JOURNEY

to crave centralized power and an established aristocracy. These were the Federalists, particularly Hamilton and Adams, who favored executive authority, admired social elites, and condemned French revolutionary manifestoes. In 1790–1791, these political differences were just beginning to solidify into what would become the first political party system in the United States—the Federalists versus the Democratic-Republicans. Even if in the aftermath of the battles over the ratification of the Constitution, the political divide in America seemed clear; decorum required that Jefferson not publicly condemn his political opponents for "heresy"—in this case Adams, whose recently published *Discourses on Davila*, featured in a Federalist New York newspaper, offered his own concerns about the French Revolution. (Privately, Jefferson had said in a letter to Madison in 1787 that Adams was a "bad calculator of the force and probable effect of the motives which govern men.")[49]

Paine's pamphlet, and Jefferson's endorsement of it, quickly consumed conversation in Philadelphia and beyond. At a soiree held by Martha Washington on May 6, 1791, only three days after *Rights of Man* appeared in bookstores, George Beckwith asked Washington's secretary, Tobias Lear, about the pamphlet. Lear thought Washington would be amused by the conversation and repeated it to the president in a letter on May 8. Beckwith expressed his concern that because the book was dedicated to Washington, the president endorsed its principles. Lear assured him that just because the book was dedicated to Washington, it did not mean he "approves of every sentiment contained in it." After all, "Upon this ground, a book containing the most wicked or absurd things might be published & dedicated to the President &c. without his Knowledge, and this dedication would be considered as his having given his sanction to them." Beckwith also mentioned that "the *Secretary of State* has given a most unequivocal sanction to the book, as Secretary of State—it is not said as Mr Jefferson." Lear responded that Jefferson certainly did not do anything he could not justify.[50]

Lear reported to Washington that Attorney General Edmund Randolph had asked Jefferson about the endorsement. Jefferson said "that he wished it might be understood that he did not authorize the publication of any part of his note." Lear advised Washington that Jefferson's published endorsement "will set him in direct opposition to Mr. Adams's political tenets." Adams had made his feeling about

26   A JOURNEY NORTH

Rights of Man clear: "I detest that book & its tendency from the bottom of my heart."[51]

The same day that Lear wrote to Washington, Jefferson did as well. He knew his endorsement had put him in the political crosshairs, and he tried to get ahead of it. He began his letter by asserting "all is well" and then promptly noted that Paine's pamphlet was beginning "to produce some squibs in our public papers." Jefferson then offered this tortured sentence in which he simultaneously avowed his friendship to Adams and denounced him for "his apostacy to hereditary monarchy and nobility." Yet "tho' we differ," he added, "we differ as friends should do."

He explained to Washington what had happened: that he was acting on Beckley's behalf and "to take off a little of the dryness of the note, I added that I was glad to find it was to be reprinted, that something would at length be publicly said against the political heresies which had lately sprung up among us." The printer included his note without permission, and Jefferson recognized that Adams "will consider me as meaning to injure him in the public eye." He added, "I am sincerely mortified to be thus brought forward on the public stage, where to remain, to advance or to retire, will be equally against my love of silence and quiet, and my abhorrence of dispute."[52]

The contretemps no doubt accelerated Jefferson's desire to get away. The next day he wrote to Madison that before departing he needed to get through a bundle of letters that required his attention and thought he would depart for New York within the week. Jefferson had invited David Rittenhouse, astronomer and president of the American Philosophical Society, to join them on the trip. Rittenhouse demurred because he could not find a good horse for the journey.

He then rehashed for Madison the story of his endorsement of Paine's pamphlet: why he wrote the note, his shock to see it printed, his opposition to Adams's *Discourses on Davila*. In addition to Adams, he conceded that Hamilton and Beckwith were "open mouthed against me." Hamilton had even accused Jefferson of being opposed to the government, "thus endeavoring to turn on the government itself those censures I meant for the enemies of the government, to wit those who want to change it into a monarchy."[53]

In his response, Madison assured Jefferson that he had suspected events unfolded just as he said and commiserated on the problem

BEFORE THE JOURNEY

of Adams, who continued to attack "the Republican Constitutions of this Country." Like Jefferson, he was dismayed by Hamilton's and Beckwith's sympathy with the British court and called it "truly ridiculous."[54]

Madison turned to the upcoming trip north and said he had no objection to Jefferson's proposed route. He mentioned that he had discussed with Beckley a trip to Boston but that it could wait.[55]

If Jefferson thought a month away would quell the controversy over *Rights of Man*, he was mistaken. Adams let it be known that he saw Jefferson's actions as electioneering and assured one correspondent that "neither Paine nor his Godfather will much effect me." He lamented Jefferson's decline in public esteem. Abigail Adams was more protective of her husband's feelings and said that she had "utter aversion" to Madison and Jefferson and could "only pitty their folly and avoid them."[56]

It was not long before Adams's feelings spilled into the emerging partisan press. A series of essays by Publicola, republished in the Federalist *Gazette of the United States*, between June and August 1791, brought what had been private considerations into open dispute. How, wondered Publicola, could Jefferson come to see *Rights of Man* as "the canonical book of political scripture" against which it was heretical to depart. It was no "Papal Bull of infallible virtue," and the citizens of the United States were free to offer a variety of opinions and challenge all orthodoxies. Respondents such as "Agricola" took umbrage at Publicola's condemnation of Jefferson and suggested that the essays were nothing less than a defense of monarchy.[57]

Many suspected that Adams himself was Publicola. Madison, however, told Jefferson the author was most likely Adams's son, twenty-three-year-old John Quincy Adams, who showed "less of clumsiness and heaviness in the stile" than in his father's writings. Madison told Jefferson that Beckley had recently returned from Boston and assured him that, even in his hometown, Adams had "become distinguished for his unpopularity." This was perhaps wishful thinking. In July 1791, Madison scrapped the idea of fulfilling his desire to travel to Boston because his horse was ill and "my bilious situation absolutely forbade it."[58]

That Madison and Jefferson did not fully appreciate the antipathy to Thomas Paine is evident from their attempt to have Washington appoint him postmaster general. In July 1791, rumors spread that

28 A JOURNEY NORTH

Samuel Osgood was planning to resign the powerful position. Madison told Jefferson, "I wish you success with all my heart in your efforts for Payne. Besides the advantage to him which he deserves, an appointment for him, at this moment would do public good in various ways." When Edmund Randolph submitted a list of possible candidates to Washington for consideration, he added Paine's name to the top. But it was not to be. Paine was still overseas and, even if he were stateside, given Federalist opposition, it is unlikely the appointment would have succeeded. Washington chose Massachusetts Federalist Timothy Pickering, who would go on to have a distinguished career as secretary of war, secretary of state, and senator from Massachusetts.[59]

Whatever his efforts on behalf of Paine, Jefferson tried to repair the rupture with Adams. He wrote the vice president, "truth, between candid minds, can never do harm." He repeated the story of how the note to the publisher had come to be and confessed that he thought so little of its import that he did not even keep a copy of it. He hoped it would attract no attention, yet on his return from his journey north with Madison he discovered the public consumed by debates over Publicola that, as a result, threw their names "on the public stage as public antagonists." Jefferson assured Adams that their differences over forms of government had always been as friends and kept in private.[60]

Adams accepted Jefferson's explanation, though not without detailing the evils that had spread from the publisher's breach of confidence. Jefferson's endorsement had been widely printed and generally seen to constitute "a direct and open personal attack upon me, by countenancing the false interpretation of my Writings as favouring the Introduction of hereditary Monarchy and Aristocracy into this Country." Adams, always sensitive to slights, had been held up "to the ridicule of the world." He concluded by saying that it was "high time" that he and Jefferson settle their differences. After fifteen years, their friendship "ever has been and Still is, very dear to my heart."[61]

Happy that their friendship was restored, Jefferson still held it against Adams that the vice president had placed so much weight on his note in *Rights of Man*. Little had been said about it until Publicola's attacks, when both Jefferson and Adams had been brought by name into the crossfire that resulted. In a reply to Adams, Jefferson protested

BEFORE THE JOURNEY 29

that he was "as innocent *in effect* as . . . in intention." Jefferson hoped
the whole business was at last over.[62]

For now, there was equanimity. It would not survive Adams's
presidency, which Jefferson would describe as a "reign of witches."
On March 4, 1801, the day of Jefferson's inauguration as president,
Adams fled Washington and did not attend the ceremonial transfer
of power.[63]

Whatever Jefferson's professed regrets over the proliferation of
partisan assaults in light of the *Rights of Man* controversy, he worked
diligently to establish a republican newspaper that would counter
John Fenno's *Gazette of the United States*, where Adams's *Discourses
on Davila* first appeared. On May 15, 1791, shortly before leaving
Philadelphia to join Madison in New York, Jefferson wrote Thomas
Mann Randolph, his son-in-law, that he considered the *Gazette of
the United States* "a paper of pure Toryism, disseminating the doctrines of monarchy, aristocracy, and the exclusion of the influence of
the people."[64]

Jefferson told Randolph that he and Madison had been trying to
establish another paper that would "furnish a whig-vehicle of intelligence." They approached Benjamin Franklin Bache to see if he
would transform his Philadelphia paper, the *General Advertiser*, into a
competing paper with the *Gazette*. Bache declined.

Jefferson also reported that they had hoped to persuade Philip
Freneau to establish a paper in Philadelphia and so far had failed.[65]
Called by some "the poet of the American Revolution," Freneau
had met Madison as a fellow student at the College of New Jersey.
He narrated his experience as a prisoner on a British man-of-war
in the Caribbean in his work *The British Prison Ship* (1781) and published his first collections of his poems in 1788. Freneau wrote for the
Freeman's Journal in Philadelphia and planned to start a rural newspaper in New Jersey. Madison thought it below his friend's talents,
and Jefferson agreed that Freneau's genius "is so superior to that of
his competitors."[66]

Madison recommended that Jefferson furnish Freneau a position
in the State Department, and on February 28, 1791, Jefferson had
written to offer a position as a translator for 250 dollars a year, a position, Jefferson assured, that "gives so little to do as not to interfere
with any other calling the person may chuse." Freneau nonetheless
declined the offer. Madison did not relent and, on May 1, wrote

30 A JOURNEY NORTH

Jefferson to say that he had seen Freneau, that Freneau on his own was regularly translating the *Leyden Gazette* from French to English, and that "being made sensible of the advantages of Philada over N. Jersey for his private undertaking, his mind is taking another turn." But Freneau never reached out to Jefferson, who told Madison on May 9, a few days before he hoped to join him in New York so that they could set out on their trip, "I suppose therefore he has changed his mind back again, for which I am really sorry."[67]

Those few days turned into more than a week. Jefferson held a meeting at the American Philosophical Society with the committee on the Hessian fly, which had been devastating wheat crops, to gather queries for his research on the insect as he traveled north with Madison. And he tried to accumulate funds. Always in debt, Jefferson asked his landlord Leiper to pay him 400 dollars for the four hogsheads of tobacco that he, Leiper, had ordered. He said he needed the money for his northward journey. While he was at it, he also told Leiper, who had agreed to have Jefferson's house painted, to have the workers ready to go at once because he did not want to smell paint upon his return. From New York, he followed up with a letter, reminding his landlord about the paint and also insisting that he install a chimney.[68]

On May 15, Jefferson informed George Washington about his impending trip. He told the president, "I shall set out tomorrow for New York, where mister Madison is waiting for me, to go up the North river [Hudson], & return down Connecticut river and through Long-island. my progress up the North river will be limited by the time I allot for my whole journey, which is a month. so that I shall turn about whenever that renders it necessary."[69]

Jefferson finally left Philadelphia with James Hemings on May 17. He noted in his account book that he heard the first whippoorwill of the season. That night he stayed in Bristol, some 20 miles outside of Philadelphia. The next day he took the Trenton ferry and visited the barber in Princeton before moving on to New Brunswick, where he spent the night. On May 19, he ferried from Elizabethtown to New York and found his way to Dorothy Ellsworth's boardinghouse at 19 Maiden Lane, where Madison was also staying (one writer called it the "best House for Company and Entertainment in the City"). Madison informed his brother, "Mr. Jefferson is here & we

BEFORE THE JOURNEY

shall set out in a day or two. The extent of our joint tour will depend on circumstances."[70]

The next morning, Jefferson and Madison had breakfast with Freneau and tried to persuade him to take a position at the State Department and become editor of a paper to rival Fenno's *Gazette*. There is no record of the conversation, and Freneau continued to resist their entreaties. Jefferson learned on his return from his journey that, once again, Freneau turned down the offer. "I am sincerely sorry that Freneau has declined coming here," Jefferson wrote Madison in July, after their trip was over. He thought Freneau's genius superior to all competitors and even said he would have given him State Department printing contracts, which would have nicely supplemented his salary. Madison must have communicated Jefferson's thought to Freneau because within a week he at last gave a "decisive answer" and agreed to come to Philadelphia and edit the newspaper. Called the *National Gazette*, its first issue appeared on October 31, 1791.[71]

In persuading Freneau to act as their surrogate and create a partisan paper that would oppose Federalist policies, Madison and Jefferson helped consolidate the very party system that they dreaded. In 1789, Jefferson wrote, "If I could not go to heaven but with a party, I would not go there at all." Much had changed in two years. Madison and Jefferson were now at the head of a faction opposed to Hamilton and Adams and their policies. They actively sought subscribers for the *National Gazette* (Madison called it a "vehicle of intelligence & entertainment"). And while Jefferson did not write directly for the newspaper, Madison did. In "The Union, Who Are Its Real Friends," which appeared March 31, 1792, Madison said real friends were not those who support debt and speculation, not those who pervert limited government by "arbitrary interpretations of insidious precedents," not those who avow monarchy and aristocracy. Rather, the real friends of the union were those who were "friends to the limited and republican system of government" and were friends to liberty. As for political parties, Madison said that since their existence could not be prevented, they must be made to check one another. By 1793, Jefferson was convinced that the paper "has saved our constitution, which was galloping fast into monarchy."[72]

32 A JOURNEY NORTH

Washington had a different view. In August 1792, he lamented to Jefferson "that internal dissensions should be harrowing & tearing our vitals." He called for greater charity for the opinions of one another and expressed his hope "that instead of wounding suspicions, & irritable charges, there may be liberal allowances—mutual forbearances—and temporising yieldings on *all sides*." If not, "the fairest prospect of happiness & prosperity that ever was presented to man, will be lost—perhaps for ever!"[73]

Jefferson replied at length. He expressed remorse about the dissension and then went on to denounce Hamilton, whose "system" "flowed from principles adverse to liberty, and was calculated to undermine and demolish the republic, by creating an influence of his department over the members of the legislature." He assured Washington that his policy was not to intermeddle with other departments (Treasury, War, the Attorney General). He complained that he had been "duped" by Hamilton into "forwarding his schemes, not then sufficiently understood by me; and of all the errors of my political life, this has occasioned me the *deepest regret*."

Jefferson defended himself against various charges made anonymously by Hamilton in Fenno's paper, among them that he started an opposition newspaper to slander the government of which he was a part. Jefferson vigorously denied the charge and said he had only seen Freneau once, at breakfast at Mrs. Ellsworth's, and that he would never "directly or indirectly, write, dictate or procure any one sentence or sentiment to be inserted *in his, or any other gazette*, to which my name was not affixed, or that of my office." It was Hamilton who besmirched the dignity of government and his office by writing anonymously for Fenno's *Gazette*. As for the papers, "No government ought to be without censors: and where the press is free, no one ever will."[74]

Jefferson took one last jab at Hamilton, and it was a sharp one: "I will not suffer my retirement to be clouded by the slanders of a man whose history, from the moment at which history can stoop to notice him, is a tissue of machinations against the liberty of the country which has not only received and given him bread, but heaped it's honors on his head."[75]

If Jefferson was trying to win over Washington, he failed. Washington again expressed his hope to see "an accommodation . . . by mutual yieldings." Allowances had to be made for one

BEFORE THE JOURNEY 33

another's opinions. He trusted that both Hamilton and Jefferson were both "pure" and "well meant" and said "experience alone will decide with respect to the salubrity of the measures wch are the subjects of dispute."[76]

Jefferson was not to be consoled. In 1793, he resigned as secretary of state. Yale president Ezra Stiles noted in his diary that Jefferson had departed "in inconcealable Disgust" and avowed never to touch a newspaper nor meddle in politics again. His second retirement would not last long. As for the *National Gazette*, Hamilton continued to harp on Freneau's paid position and asked whether the patronage position was created "to oppose the measures of government, and by false insinuations, to disturb the public peace?" By 1794, in the aftermath of the yellow fever outbreak in Philadelphia, the paper was no more.[77]

Madison and Jefferson's northern journey came in the midst of these political battles. Suspicious Federalists thought the two were engaged in "a passionate courtship" of political allies such as Chancellor Robert Livingston, a prominent New York attorney whom one day Jefferson would appoint minister to France, and Aaron Burr, who earlier in the year had defeated Philip Schuyler and was elected senator from New York. Jefferson and Madison dined with them before the start of the trip. Robert Troup, a New York lawyer and future judge, told Hamilton, "Delenda est Carthago [Carthage must be destroyed] I suppose is the Maxim adopted with respect to you. They had better be quiet, for if they succeed they will tumble the fabric of the government in ruins to the ground."[78]

British diplomats and spies, allies of Hamilton and the Federalists, also saw something sinister in the trip. John Temple, British general consul, warned that Jefferson and Madison had "gone to the Eastern States, there to prosleyte as far as they are able to a commercial war with Great Britain." On learning of Jefferson and Madison's plans for the journey, George Beckwith, British army officer, agent, and spy, undertook a counter-tour of New England to bolster the "critical conditions of the Empire in the country," and reported to Lord Grenville, Britain's foreign secretary, that his entreaties were well met.[79]

No question, politics was on everyone's mind. Jefferson and Madison's tour through Federalist New England undoubtedly reinforced for them the necessity of taking a firm public stand against what they saw as the heresies of the day. Yet, in the end, politics was not their main purpose. They sought relief from the physical ailments that afflicted them; they sought a change of scenery, a jaunt through a fresh landscape; they sought information about a destructive insect. "Health, recreation, and curiosity," said Madison. Together, they were on their way.[80]

The Journey

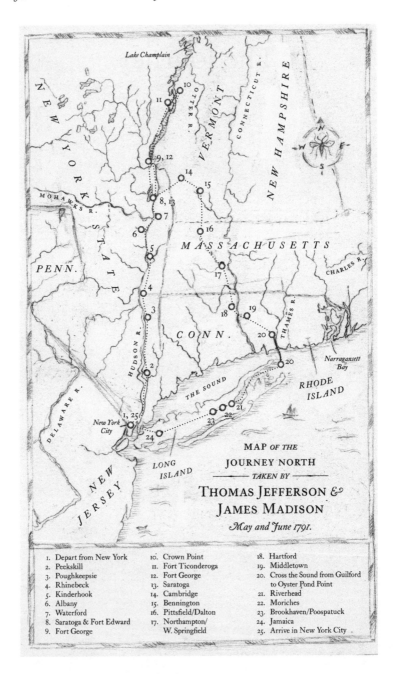

At Poughkeepsie: The Hessian Fly (May 23)

Ready to leave New York, Thomas Jefferson sent James Hemings ahead to Poughkeepsie with his phaeton—a light, open carriage—and his and Madison's horses. There is no record of whether Madison was accompanied by a servant, though it seems unlikely that he was not. A man named Sawney, an enslaved person at Montpelier, accompanied Madison to Princeton when he attended college, and another named Billey attended Madison in Philadelphia at the Confederation Congress. In all likelihood, Hemings served both men. But it is also possible that a servant named Matthew accompanied Madison. If so, it might have been Matthew Lavoratorini, who had labored for Jefferson in some capacity from July 1790 to April 1791. Matthew, also called "Matteo," wanted to leave Philadelphia for New York. An ad for his replacement, placed by Jefferson in the *Philadelphia Daily Advertiser*, read, "Wanted, A Genteel Servant, who can shave and dress well, attend a gentleman on horseback, wait at table, and be well recommended." Matthew may have made his way to New York, where, perhaps with a recommendation from Jefferson, he somehow ended up with Madison. Clearly, there was some connection because, several months after returning from their trip, Madison informed Jefferson that he planned to leave Matthew in Philadelphia on his trip from New York to Virginia.

Whatever the precise circumstances, the journey on which Jefferson and Madison were about to embark included an enslaved man and perhaps a servant. Once the ship sailed, however, there is no mention of either. It is a resounding silence in the record, repeated

38   A JOURNEY NORTH

over and over again in history: people who were present but not considered.[1]

On Saturday, May 21, Jefferson and Madison boarded Captain John Cooper's sloop for the trip up the Hudson. Jefferson paid 6.86 dollars for passage to Poughkeepsie, and the men arrived there two days later. In his journal, he commented on the white pine, pitch-pine, and juniper trees. The first night was spent at Conklin's Tavern, located above Peekskill, and the next night at Hendrickson's Market Street Tavern, which he judged as "good." Throughout the journey, Jefferson kept a chart and rated the inns good, middling, or bad.

A few years earlier, journeying through France, Jefferson captured the romance of passing a night at an inn. From Marseilles, he wrote that a traveler "retired at night to his chamber in an Inn, all his effects contained in a single trunk, all his cares circumscribed by the walls of his apartment, unknown to all, unheeded, and undisturbed, writes, reads, thinks, sleeps, just in the moments when nature and the movements of his body and mind require. Charmed with the tranquility of his little cell, he finds how few are our real wants, how cheap a thing is happiness." It is enough to make one want to travel.[2]

George Washington was much less dreamy about being on the road. In 1789, as president, he visited New England and, two years later, toured the South (for part of that jaunt, he was traveling at the same time as Jefferson and Madison). As noted earlier, Washington set out to visit every state during his term in office, both to win support for the new federal government and "to become better acquainted with their principal Characters & internal Circumstances." Wanting to represent republican simplicity, he stayed at inns or public houses, not private homes, and often found them wanting. He recorded his impressions in his diary: an "ordinary house," "indifferent house," "not a Good house." (At best, he labeled some "pretty good" or "decent.") The houses could be small, the beds uncomfortable, the stables insufficient, the food unappetizing. The New England roads were no better—Washington described them as "rough," "stoney," "uneven." He liked the road from Hartford to Springfield, though even here he wrote that while it was "level & good," it was "too Sandy in places." Whether in carriage or on horseback, travelers had to endure as much as enjoy the miles they covered. The distances added up quickly. During their trip, Jefferson and Madison would average 30 miles a day.[3]

AT POUGHKEEPSIE: THE HESSIAN FLY (MAY 23) 39

On May 24, Jefferson and Madison breakfasted and dined at Lasher's inn, which Jefferson rated as "good." He spoke with the proprietor, Conrad Lasher, a former Revolutionary War soldier, and for the first of many times along the way, he asked about the Hessian fly, which he saw in the stubble after a wheat harvest. If there was a single purpose for the northern journey from Jefferson's perspective, it was to conduct research on the fly, a topic that preoccupied him, as well as Madison and many others, including Washington.

Jefferson studied all aspects of natural history: insects, birds, plants, flowers, fossils. The Hessian fly—*Mayetiola destructor*—in particular held a special place in his scientific inquiries. Political opponents took pleasure in mocking him for his interest in insects. One Federalist imagined him penning "a dissertation on cockroaches." Washington Irving pictured Jefferson amusing himself by "impaling butterflies and pickling tadpoles."[4]

Let them ridicule, Jefferson thought. Nothing pleased him more than scientific inquiry, and he would have happily surrendered his political life, he wrote in 1792, for "retirement to my own home and my own affairs." His study of the Hessian fly allowed temporary escape from partisan politics at a volatile moment.[5]

The Hessian fly appeared in America at the time of the Revolution. It is small (about one-eighth-inch long) and reddish brown to black. As an adult, the fly lives only a few days and is harmless. In its larval stage, however, the insect devastates wheat, which it prefers to barley and rye (for unknown reasons it avoids oats). In the fall, adult females lay several hundred eggs in the grooves of the wheat leaves low on the plant, and the larvae that emerge feed off the wheat until cold weather arrives. Come spring, adult flies lay eggs on the leaves, and a new generation of larvae destroys the stalks. Typically, there are two cycles in the North; as many as five in the South. Though discovered in the late eighteenth century, the fly continues to pose a threat to wheat growers, and various strategies of management, including crop rotation and the use of insecticides, have sought to keep infestations under control.

George Morgan, a prominent Revolutionary, who farmed several hundred acres of land near Princeton, described the fly in 1788: "White Worms which after a few days turn of a Chesnut Colour—They are deposited by a Fly between the Leaves & the Stalk of the green Wheat & generally at the lower-most Joint, and

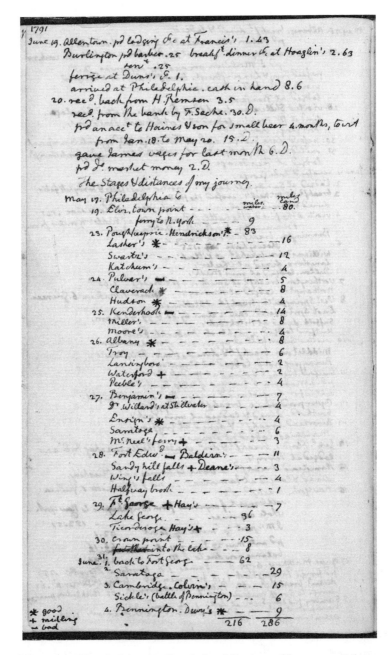

Figure 2 Jefferson's Distance Traveled and Ratings of Inns, 1791 (Library of Congress)

AT POUGHKEEPSIE: THE HESSIAN FLY (MAY 23) 41

are inevitable Death to the Stalks they attack." Modern agricultural techniques control the infestation by changing planting dates and using resistant varieties of wheat. In post-Revolutionary America, farmers were desperate to understand the destructive insect as they watched it advance from Brooklyn and Long Island, where it was first discovered.[6]

By 1787, journals, newspapers, and correspondence were filled with references to the Hessian fly; its name derived from the belief that it arrived buried in the straw beds of mercenary Hessian soldiers disembarking in New York to fight on the side of Great Britain. In a letter written in 1788 to John Temple, British Consul-General George Morgan took credit for the name:

> The name of *Hessian* Fly was given to this Insect by myself. . . .
> We agreed to use some Industry in spreading the name to add,
> if possible to the detestation in which the human was generally
> held by our yeomanry & to hand it down with all possible Infamy
> to the next generation as a useful National Prejudice. It is now
> become the most opprobrious Term our Language affords & the
> greatest affront our Chimney Sweepers & even our Slaves can
> give or receive, is to call or be called *Hessian*.[7]

Some 30,000 Hessians fought for the British during the war. The Declaration of Independence condemned their depredations and denounced the king for "transporting large Armies of foreign Mercenaries to compleat the works of death, desolation and tyranny." Hatred of the Hessian soldiers was so intense that some went even further. An anonymous jeremiad published in 1788 speculated that the soldiers had carried the insects intentionally, as a form of biological warfare: "the Hessians have brought over thousands of little *insects*, on purpose to destroy this country." The fly's origins would come to be debated, yet one thing was certain: long after the war ended, the fly remained. "The little Enemy dwells in safety," William Hay, a Richmond merchant, wrote to Jefferson in April 1787.[8] Hay warned that farmers in Virginia "have been obliged to leave off the Culture of wheat, and by that Means, have left their farms."

Madison first communicated with Jefferson about the fly in a post-script to a July 1788 letter about the ratification of the Constitution. He informed him that "the destructive insect which goes under the

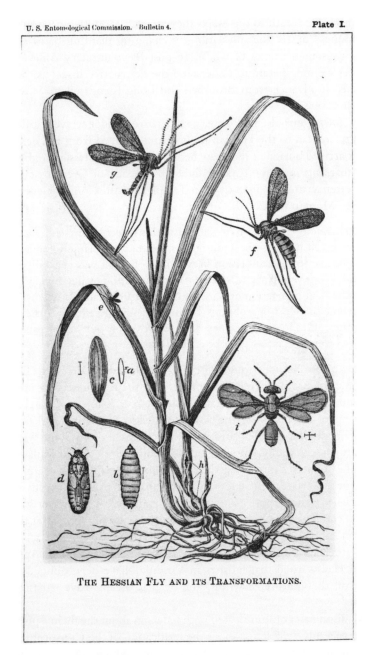

Figure 3 Hessian Fly from A. S. Packard, *The Hessian Fly: Its Ravages, Habits, Enemies and Means of Preventing Its Increase* (Washington, DC: Government Printing Office, 1880)

name of the Hessian fly . . . seems to be making an annual progress in every direction." Writing from Mount Vernon in August 1788, George Washington expressed his concern about the "ravages of the Hessian fly on the wheaten Crops in the States East of the Delaware and of the progress of this destructive insect Southerly." His anxiety may have been fueled by a letter he had received the previous month from Richard Peters, a member of the Pennsylvania House of Representatives (Washington would one day nominate him to the United States District Court), who wrote "as to Wheat with us it is pretty near at an End. The Hessian Fly is now within 10 Miles of us & next Year we shall have it lay us all Waste. This seems as great a Curse as the British Army was, if not greater. We could combat their other Hessian Auxiliaries; but this is unconquerable."[9]

Agriculture was never far from the minds of Washington, Jefferson, and Madison, and they were particularly concerned about wheat. Washington called agriculture "my favourite amusement." A long letter from Madison to Jefferson in 1786, in which he contemplated the relationship among forms of government, population, and misery, also reported that farmers had lost their crops of wheat. When Jefferson wrote to Washington in May 1789, to congratulate him on his election as president, he included extracts from a letter from Thomas Paine, stating that England's Privy Council was considering a ban on wheat imports because of the "American fly."[10]

The threat of the Hessian fly was particularly unnerving to Virginian planters and farmers because the post-Revolutionary economy accelerated movement away from tobacco production to diversification in grain crops. During the war, tobacco production dropped markedly in Virginia, from 55 million pounds to 14.5 million in the first year alone, primarily from a decline in exports. The shift, however, had begun earlier, primarily from soil exhaustion. Washington's experience was emblematic. Between 1763 and 1773, production of tobacco dropped from nearly 90,000 pounds to almost nothing. By contrast, in 1787, his farms yielded 10,000 bushels of wheat. The price of tobacco steadily declined, while wheat prices increased. And unlike some other crops, wheat was both a commercial crop and one that provided subsistence to the grower. It is little wonder the Hessian fly generated enormous anxiety.[11]

The movement away from tobacco and the cultivation of wheat also fit with the ideals of the new nation itself. In one of the queries in his *Notes on the State of Virginia* (1785), Jefferson argued in favor of wheat over tobacco. The one "diffuses plenty and happiness among the whole"; the other creates a "culture productive of infinite wretchedness" that impoverishes the laborer as well as the earth itself. He thought "it easier to make a hundred bushels of wheat than a thousand weight of tobacco, and they are worth more when made." Jefferson addressed the problem of the weevil—a long-snouted beetle—and thought it manageable; the Hessian fly was still largely unknown. He probably first learned of the "pernicious insect" from a letter received in April 1787.[12]

Americans tried to cope with the pestilence and devise farming strategies to defeat it. In February 1787, the *American Museum*, a monthly magazine launched that year in Philadelphia that included such notable subscribers as Benjamin Franklin, Washington, Jefferson, and Madison, contained an article on the Hessian fly. The writer noted that since its discovery on Long Island, the fly's reach had extended 15–20 miles a year. Farmers watched its approach with dread, knowing that "unless means are discovered to prevent its progress, the whole continent will be over-run—a calamity more to be lamented than the ravages of war."[13]

One writer suggested that the use of elder leaves, with their disagreeable odor, might be infused into water and sprinkled over the wheat's ridges. Another wondered if certain weeds might prove noxious to the fly. A farmer from New Jersey pointed out that the flies appear in September and recommended waiting until October to sow. In spring, when they appear as small worms, perhaps a roller drawn over the wheat would crush them. Desperate for a solution, a writer from New York suggested sprinkling salt on the wheat in the mistaken belief that wheat sown on land near the ocean does better than wheat sown inland.[14]

In June 1787, the *American Museum* published an address by George Morgan to the Philadelphia Society for Promoting Agriculture. Morgan had heard rumors that some farmers on Long Island were using a species of wheat that the flies did not disturb. Writing from New Jersey, Morgan reported that the fly did not arrive in his area until May 1786 and had increased to such a degree that some farmers plowed over their fields and planted rye, though it was unclear whether the fly was equally destructive of other grains. Morgan experimented with rolling his fields and was convinced doing so destroyed the fly in its chrysalis state. He called on the society for more study and concluded with the request to borrow a microscope.[15]

Morgan must have acquired the instrument because a few months later he added to his remarks and observed that the fly initially appears as white with long black legs and whiskers before it turns black. He warned against opening a window and lighting a candle at night. He did so and discovered "without exaggeration . . . that a glass tumbler from which beer had just been drunk, at dinner, had five hundred flies in it, within a few minutes."[16]

A farmer on Long Island informed Morgan that yellow-bearded wheat, not red- or white-bearded, had been found to resist the fly. The beard refers to the material that protects the kernel. Morgan spread the gospel and declared "as a lover of my country, and friend to farmers" that they must rely on yellow- and not white- or red-bearded wheat. He communicated this finding directly to George Washington and sent him a wheat sample. Washington praised Morgan for his efforts and acknowledged, "If the yellow bearded wheat from a continuation of experiments is found no matter from what cause, to be obnoxious to and able to withstand this all devouring insect [it] must indeed be valuable." Washington spread the word, telling one agriculturist, "*White Wheat* must yield the palm to the *yellow bearded*, which alone, it seems, is able to resist the depredations of that destructive insect." A year later, Washington was still preaching the gospel that yellow-bearded wheat alone could resist "the ravages of this . . . all conquering foe." While yellow-bearded wheat proved more fly-resistant and farmers and millers in the mid–Atlantic embraced it, the switch did not help Washington. By 1794, the fly was in the wheat at Mt. Vernon.[17]

The fly not only threatened starvation to farmers, it also endangered the nation's commercial interests and reputation abroad. Grain exports in wheat and flour were central to America's transatlantic commerce. This soon came under threat as reports on the fly and warnings about importing American wheat reached London. In April 1788, Phineas Bond, British consul at Philadelphia, informed Lord Carmarthen, the foreign secretary, that "an insect called the Hessian fly, whose ravages have been progressive, and in some instances ruinous," probably deposits its eggs in the grain. He expressed his fear that imports of American wheat would introduce the insect to other grains and prove fatal to the "agriculture of the

Kingdom." Carmarthen also heard from Joseph Banks, president of the Royal Society of London and scientific adviser to the Privy Council for Trade. Banks similarly believed the insect was present in the grain and warned that the introduction of the fly through imports of American wheat would "be an evil of the most dreadful nature." In June 1788, England's Privy Council recommended to King George that he issue a proclamation banning imports of American wheat. The following year Benjamin Vaughan, politician and physician, writing from London, informed his brother John Vaughan, a merchant and philanthropist living in Philadelphia, that he had seen the report on insects presented to the House of Commons. The report, he wrote, was so unfavorable that imports might be "wholly interdicted."[18]

Jefferson was concerned. "Can you inform me what has been done by England on the subject of our wheat and flour?" he wrote in October 1788 to John Brown Cutting, lawyer, agent, and all-around London gossip. Cutting responded that ministerial motives were always inscrutable and thought that in this case the ban was motivated by "an envious malignant disposition that is gratified in puny efforts to fetter the commerce and check the prosperity of a country whom it cannot forgive because it cou'd not subdue." The Duke of Grafton gave support to this view. He called the fly "a scourge of Heaven . . . upon such ungratefull colonies and rebellious people." Jefferson also heard from Thomas Paine, who said he explained to Banks that "the Hessian fly attacked only the green plant, and did not exist in the dry grain." Paine said it was "old News" that "the King is insane," and thought the ban was "only a political manoeuvre of the Ministry."[19]

American farmers and merchants communicated their anxiety to George Washington, who heard from Samuel Powel, a prominent Philadelphia politician, that Pennsylvania's Executive Council had prepared a report that showed it was the plant, and not the grain, that was at risk from the fly. "The Propagation of this Scourge cannot happen," the report concluded, "from sowing wheat that has grown on Land infested by this animal." "If the insect they pretend to fear is the Hessian fly," wrote Jefferson, "it never existed in the grain."[20]

Jefferson saw England's actions as "a libel on our wheat." Prior to the Revolution, England imported more than 50,000 quarters of wheat (a quarter was one-quarter ton) from the American colonies.

AT POUGHKEEPSIE: THE HESSIAN FLY (MAY 23)   47

That fell to 9,000 in the early 1780s, but it was on the rise again. Jefferson did not believe the Crown's actions stemmed from a real fear of introducing the fly. Rather, it was England's blatant attempt to denigrate the United States. The prohibition, Jefferson lamented, "can have no object but to do us injury by spreading a groundless alarm in those countries of Europe where our wheat is constantly and kindly received. It is a mere assassination."[21]

That England reversed course in 1790 suggests Jefferson had a point. British leaders acknowledged that the Hessian fly posed no danger to imports—cargo inspectors reported no sign of the insect—and harvest failures in England made the nation more dependent than ever on imports. The storming of the Bastille and other events in France, where Jefferson was serving as American minister in Paris, no doubt added to royal anxiety about making certain there was an abundance of grain: Parisians suffered food shortages.

Jefferson needed little incentive to despise the British as much as the Hessian fly. In 1785, he wrote Abigail Adams that he considered London's residents a collection of "rich, proud, hectoring, swearing, squibbing, carnivorous animals." He returned from France in November 1789 and learned of his appointment as secretary of state in Washington's Cabinet. Although he would be consumed by politics, the Hessian fly continued to hold his attention.[22]

Others, too, became preoccupied with the fly, notably Samuel Latham Mitchill. Born in New York in 1764, Mitchill was educated in medicine at the University of Edinburgh. On his return to the United States in 1786, he immersed himself in the study of natural history. He also studied law and impressed others with his remarkable memory and wide-ranging interests. Some even compared him to Franklin.[23] In 1788, Mitchill published "An Account of the Insect." He began his essay with a defense of "the contemplation of small matters" and chided those who would mock the botanist who climbed a mountain in search of a bit of moss. He hoped that his observations might help avoid a national calamity. Much of what he said was quickly becoming common knowledge: that the fly appeared in 1776, that the eggs produce larvae that attack the stalks, and that no method had yet been discovered to eradicate the insect. The best hope, he thought, was to delay autumnal planting until cold had set in.[24]

48   A JOURNEY NORTH

Mitchill's most important contribution was to the discussion of the origins of the Hessian fly. He questioned the story that Hessian soldiers had brought the fly in their bedding, noting that Americans were "ever fond of ascribing every thing disagreeable to the Germans." "It must be highly improbable," he reasoned, "that an insect, ingesting only green and growing wheat, should be imported from a land, whence neither plants, nor grains, nor straw, nor chaff, as far as I know, ever arrived." Sir Joseph Banks, president of the Royal Society in London, assured Mitchill that the insect was unknown in England and had never been observed in Germany. Mitchill also reviewed Francesco Gianni's *Delle Mallattie del Grano in Erba* (*On Diseases of Grain in Grass*) and found in Italy nothing that resembled the "American wheat-insect." He concluded that the fly "has long been a resident in our territories" and only lately found in wheat a "new repository for his destructive progeny." A consensus was emerging. The fly was "an entirely American production." By the nineteenth century, one observer reported "it is now generally believed to be a native of America."[25]

Not everyone reacted scientifically. While we think of the era as an age of enlightenment and reason, post-Revolutionary America also contained its share of religious prophetic voices who condemned the infidelity of the age and warned of God's punishment. Timothy Dwight, Congregationalist minister and president of Yale from 1795 to 1817, thundered that "the army of God, which has humbled the pride, frustrated the designs, and annihilated the hopes of man" had as its soldiers the "*Canker-worm, the Caterpillar, the Palmer-worm, and the Locust.*" The Hessian fly, he observed, was smaller than a gnat and defenseless, yet it wrought havoc on the nation. Another writer, calling himself The Prophet Nathan, or Plain Friend, considered the Hessian fly "a judgment upon the land." The fly, averred the writer, was "*commissioned by the Almighty to cut off the staff of life*; as a testimony of his displeasure against the *wickedness* of this land." That wickedness included a clamor for commercial profits and the bitter partisan politics of which Jefferson and Madison were very much a part. "The mighty army of the fly" was spreading desolation. "Before these powerful armies, nature is smiling in all its bloom and pride."[26]

Jefferson had a different view of nature. It was not an agent of God's wrath and providence. Rather, it was subject to discoverable laws, the "laws of nature and nature's God." He became formally involved in investigating the Hessian fly when he made a motion on April 15, 1791, to the American Philosophical Society to create a committee for those purposes. Jefferson was elected to membership in 1780 and served as president from 1797 to 1814. He chaired the Hessian fly committee, whose other members included the botanist Benjamin Smith Barton, physician James Hutchinson, anatomist Caspar Wistar, and Charles Thomson, who had served as secretary of the Continental Congress for fifteen years. The committee sought to study "the natural History of the insect usually called the Hessian fly" and determine "the best means of preventing and destroying" it. On May 1, Jefferson wrote his son-in-law, Thomas Mann Randolph, Jr., that a committee to collect materials on the natural history of the Hessian fly had been created and suggested that Randolph turn his attention to the insect. Jefferson added, "I long to be free for pursuits of this kind instead of the detestable ones in which I am now labouring without pleasure to myself, or profit to others."[27]

He soon freed himself precisely for that pursuit when he and Madison left on their journey. He had told committee members on May 12, 1791, of his plans to "leave town on Sunday for a month, to set out on a journey which will carry him through N. York and the whole of Long island, where this animal has raged much," and hoped Barton would have prepared queries by then for him to present. Those queries would be published as a circular on April 17, 1792, and included such questions as when did the fly appear; in what state, egg or worm; what kind of wheat did it attack; and what practices have been found to be successful in combating the insect.[28]

Jefferson's most extensive writing during the tour with Madison was his notes on the Hessian fly. He was a diligent entomologist, asking everyone he met for information that he jotted down in his field notes. After his first conversation with Conrad Lasher, he reviewed the morphology of the insect and noted that he had seen it in its worm state days earlier—"white, smooth and transparent." Lasher counted 120 worms on one stalk. Attempts to add manure ("highly dunging a piece of ground") to strengthen the wheat had no effect. "They are never in the grain or chaff," Jefferson wrote, no doubt thinking of the Privy Council's preposterous ban on wheat imports.[29]

Jefferson paid careful attention to the dates when crops were attacked. In this region above Poughkeepsie, the fly arrived in 1785

50 A JOURNEY NORTH

and destroyed the entire crop in 1786, 1787, and 1788. Lasher tried a new white-bearded wheat and had no insects in 1790 or so far in 1791. Elsewhere the story remained the same. Jefferson noted the fly attacked rye a little and oats hardly at all. In Albany, Jefferson spoke with Philip Schuyler, who reported some destruction in 1787 and 1788 (maybe one-tenth of the crop), but nothing in 1790 nor that year so far.

Schuyler was the most prominent political figure Jefferson and Madison met during the trip. He had served in the Continental Congress and as a major general during the war. A wealthy landowner and slaveowner, Schuyler supported the Constitution, and the state legislature elected him senator from New York in the First Congress. In January 1791, Schuyler lost reelection to Aaron Burr, who in time became a prominent Democratic-Republican. Burr's victory unleashed the ongoing hostility with Hamilton (Schuyler was his father-in-law) that would lead to the fatal duel in 1804.

Albany was one of the few cities where newspapers noted the visit. The *Albany Register* observed, "on Thursday last this city was honored with the presence of Mr. Jefferson, secretary of state, accompanied by the *Charles Fox* of America, the celebrated Madison. We are informed they are going north, as far as Lake Champlain, and then across the *fifteenth Constellation*, east to Connecticut river." Fox was a Whig politician in the House of Commons steadfastly opposed to Tory policies. The reference would have been clear to readers of the paper, which opposed Federalist dogma and saw Madison as a leader of the Democratic-Republican.[30]

A few weeks later, a paper in Vermont published under an Albany dateline of May 30 an item that regretted that the short stay of Jefferson and Madison in the city "deprived our principal characters from paying that respectful attention due to their distinguished merit." The commentary praised "these enlightened patriots" for exploring the country, much as George Washington, who had just completed a lengthy tour of the southern states. Unlike Jefferson and Madison's northern tour, Washington's southern journey was entirely political. He drew crowds and made speeches. In Georgia, he even met with several Catawba chiefs to discuss treaties.

Despite the differences in the journeys, the writer thought the actions of these men contrasted with eastern Federalist leaders who are "wallowing in every species of dissipation, regardless of the

AT POUGHKEEPSIE: THE HESSIAN FLY (MAY 23) 51

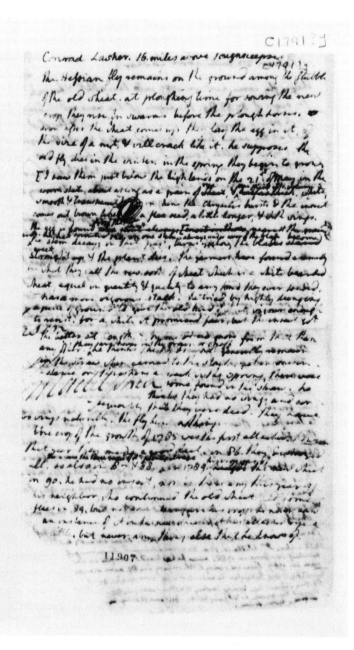

Figure 4 Jefferson's Notes on the Hessian Fly, 1791 (Library of Congress)

52   A JOURNEY NORTH

happiness or prosperity of their country." Rather, those like Jefferson and Madison were "industriously prying into an accurate knowledge of the situation of every part of the union from personal observation. With such men at the helm we passengers can promise ourselves nothing less than a prosperous and pleasant voyage."[31]

It is unlikely that the meeting with Schuyler touched directly on politics in any way. Jefferson was focused on the Hessian fly, and Schuyler's estate covered thousands of acres. Moreover, whatever Jefferson's feeling about Schuyler's son-in-law, he was enraptured by his married daughter Angelica, whom he had met in Paris and with whom he sustained a flirtatious correspondence. They exchanged books and trinkets. (Jefferson's copy of the *Federalist Papers* was the edition signed by Eliza Hamilton and given to her sister.) He suggested that the two of them travel together and, in one letter, mentioned her father. Jefferson wrote from Paris in 1788, "I will flatter myself with the hope of seeing you at New York, or even at Albany if I am master enough of my time. To see the country will be one motive: but to see you a much stronger, and to become acquainted with your father who must be good, because you are so. The fruit is a specimen of the tree. I had the honour of serving with him in Congress in the year 1775. but probably he does not remember me." Botanical fruit was not the only kind that interested Jefferson.[32]

Leaving Albany on May 27, Jefferson and Madison visited Cohoes Falls, a dramatic waterfall along the Mohawk River. Named by the Iroquois, Cohoes meant "canoe falling." Eighteenth-century travelers marveled at the cascade of falling water, which drops 90 feet from its heights. Marquis de Chastellux, visiting a decade before Jefferson and Madison, called it "a vast sheet of water, . . . one of the wonders of America." Jefferson, however, seemed unimpressed. He measured the Falls at 70 feet, and in a letter to his son-in-law, written from Vermont on June 5, expressed greater appreciation for Wing's Falls and Sandy Hills Falls, located in present-day Glenn Falls and Hudson Falls, New York. Those he called "two very remarkable cataracts." The geology interested him more than the vista, and he speculated that the bed of the Cohoes on the west side of the Hudson was not limestone, whereas on the east side it was. Perhaps he was uninspired by the Cohoes because in Virginia he had visited Falling Spring Falls, which he believed fell some 200 feet into a valley below.

AT POUGHKEEPSIE: THE HESSIAN FLY (MAY 23) 53

Still, he thought it noteworthy enough to mention in his memorandum book.[33]

They also toured several manufacturers. One exported 1,000 barrels of herring annually; a distiller shipped 1,000 hogsheads of rum annually. Jefferson was especially taken with a nailery he visited: "Saw nails made by cutting them with a pair of shears from the end of a bar of iron, the thickness of which corresponded with the thickness of the nail, and its breadth with the length. We saw 120. cut off in a minute, and 24. headed in a minute, which would amount to 20. a minute cut off and headed. But they make habitually about 4000. a day." A few years later, Jefferson added a nailery at Monticello, and his enslaved nail makers (boys aged ten to sixteen) produced as many as 10,000 nails a day by 1795. Isaac Jefferson, an enslaved worker at the nailery, recalled that Jefferson imported from England a nail-cutting machine, and he "gave the boys in the nail-factory a pound of meat a week, a dozen herrings, a quart of molasses & peck of meal." The hardest-working ones were rewarded with a new suit of clothes. During one of his brief retirements from politics, in 1794, he wrote, "I am so much immersed in farming and nail-making (for I have set up a Nailery) that politicks are entirely banished from my mind."[34]

However much manufacturing mattered, farming came first, and at every stop along the journey Jefferson continued his inquiries about the fly. The consensus was that while it had damaged crops a few years earlier, for some reason its depredations had abated. Some information was contradictory. In Southold, on Long Island, farmers thought the use of additional manure helped. A new white wheat seemed even more resistant than the yellow-bearded wheat. Jefferson noted that the fly first appeared in Flatbush and traveled about 20 miles a year based on prevailing winds, yet it "cannot go Westardly because repelled by the Westardly winds." In South Amboy, New Jersey, on his way back to Philadelphia, Jefferson received a less optimistic report. "They fluctuate, prevailing less some years, more the next," he was told. "This year they will destroy two-thirds." And the bearded wheat was also attacked, though less vigorously. Jefferson found some cocoons, and on his return from the journey continued his investigations into the fly. He asked Madison, who was considering a trip to Boston, a trip he never made, that he "continue the inquiries relative to the Hessian fly, and note them."[35]

54 A JOURNEY NORTH

That August, at a meeting of the American Philosophical Society, Jefferson heard Samuel Mitchill's report and received follow-up letters from people he had spoken with during the journey. Jonathan Havens, who would soon publish *Observations on the Hessian Fly* (1792), and Sylvester Dering, who Jefferson called "particularly serious on his observations on this fly," wrote at great length and reported "the fly has again increased in the present year so as to be found in great plenty in many places." Jefferson must have been thrilled in September to receive from Ezra L'Hommedieu, a New York lawyer and former delegate to the Continental Congress, a packet of stubble of yellow-bearded wheat. L'Hommedieu wrote, "By carefully examining this Stubble, by opening the Straw near the Roots and first Joints you will find many of the Insects in their chrysalis State still alive and their Inclosure or Case very Tender."[36]

In June 1792, Jefferson again received several stalks of wheat with, as he noted, "the Chrysalis of the Hessian fly in them." While we do not know what he did with the first sample, this time he studied the fly closely, no doubt under a microscope. He observed it was between the size of a gnat and a mosquito. He looked at the head, eyes, and trunk. He examined the penis. The wings, he wrote, were "membraneous" and "divided into three compartments by two strong nerves running longitudinally."[37]

Jefferson reported his findings to his son-in-law: "We have an opportunity now of examining this insect well. I have several of them now hatching. The examination of a single one which hatched a week ago, gives me reason to suspect they are non-descript, and consequently aboriginal here."[38]

Jefferson continued to receive letters about the Hessian fly and responses to the American Philosophical Society Committee queries, but his attention drifted elsewhere. When he replied to correspondents, his acknowledgment was cursory and polite. The Committee never issued a report. Perhaps he thought the subject had been well covered by others. Perhaps evidence of decline of the insect in 1791 led him to lose any sense of urgency. No doubt his responsibilities as secretary of state and battles with Alexander Hamilton and the Federalists absorbed most of his energy.

By the mid-1790s, with the fly entrenched in Delaware and Eastern Maryland, the mid-Atlantic centers of grain production, and with commercial relations with England and France interrupted, wheat exports plummeted. It had been a million bushels a year before 1792 and then fell precipitously to as low as thirty thousand bushels in 1795. Many Northern farmers, in New Jersey, New York, and Connecticut, abandoned wheat cultivation altogether. Economic historians have shown how the Hessian fly transformed grain culture in the late eighteenth century, leading to experiments with crop diversification and adoption of new methods—such as delayed planting—to combat the consequences. Wheat cultivation moved south, and the insect did as well. The architect Benjamin Latrobe visited Washington at Mt. Vernon in July 1796 and recorded in his journal that, during a long conversation, he "gave me a very minute account of the Hessian fly and its progress from Long Island, where it first appeared. . . . It has not yet appeared in Virginia, but is daily dreaded."[39]

In an oration delivered in 1798 before the Academy of Medicine in Philadelphia, the physician Charles Caldwell remarked, "it will take many years to obliterate from the memory" of farmers "the injuries they have sustained from the invasion and ravages of the Hessian fly."[40]

If Jefferson abandoned the fly, the fly did not abandon him. Writing from Washington on November 16, 1801, the newly inaugurated president noted that "the Hessian fly is laying waste [to] all the wheat in this quarter." He informed Secretary of State James Monroe, his Albemarle County neighbor, "the Hessian fly appears alarmingly in our growing crop." He wrote to Madison in 1813, "We have never seen so unpromising a crop of wheat as that now growing. the winter killed an unusual proportion of it, and the fly is destroying the remainder." A few years later, in 1817, he lamented "we, of this state, must make bread, and be contented with so much of that as a miserable insect will leave us. this remnant will scarcely feed us the present year, for such swarms of the Wheat-fly were never before seen in this country."[41]

Madison, too, reported to correspondents on the fly's depredations, which had first found its way to his plantation in 1798. Madison told Jefferson, "You will do well in making your arrangements for the arrival of the Hessian fly among you next season." A decade later, he wrote that "the crop of wheat, tho' shortened, will be tolerable, in tolerable land, where the Hessians have not committed their ravages." In 1824, he offered a pithy summary of the catastrophe: "no defence agst the Hessian fly the great enemy to our wheat crops."[42]

Long after the northern tour had ended, the Hessian fly continued to command their attention.

At Fort George: Prince Taylor (June 1)

On May 29, Jefferson and Madison boarded a ship and sailed the length of Lake George, which Jefferson estimated as 36 miles long (he was close—it is 32.2 miles). The body of water acquired its name in 1755, during the French and Indian War, when William Johnson, the head of British forces, renamed it in honor of King George from its French name, Lac du Saint-Sacrement, given in 1646. The Mohawk and Onondoga tribes that lived in the area for centuries called it Andia-ta-roc-te ("the lake that shuts itself in"). On May 31, Jefferson wrote his daughter Martha, "Lake George is without comparison the most beautiful water I ever saw."[1]

Although the swarms of mosquitoes and gnats were annoying, the men clearly enjoyed themselves. They fished in the clear waters and saw salmon trout, speckled or red trout, Oswego bass, rock bass, and yellow perch. They noted seagulls, loons, and wild ducks. At one point, they killed two rattlesnakes "of a sutty dark colour, obscurely checkered." They also hunted red squirrel. (Jefferson once advised his nephew, "let your gun . . . be the constant companion of your walks.") He informed Thomas Mann Randolph, "We have met with a small red squirrel, of the colour of our fox squirrel with a black stripe on each side, weighing about six ounces generally, and in such abundance, on Lake Champlain particularly, as that twenty odd were killed at the house we lodged in opposite Crown point the morning we arrived there, without going ten steps from the door. We killed three which were crossing the lakes, one of them just as he was getting ashore where it was three miles wide, and where, with the high winds then blowing, he must have made it 5 or 6 miles."[2]

Madison noted "the mountains of considerable height the entire length of the lake." Jefferson observed in his journal that one of the rock formations was "famous" for having been the site of a daring escape by a man named Rogers who eluded Indians by "sliding down it when covered with snow, and escaping across the lake then frozen over."[3]

Jefferson knew his history. What he alluded to in his journal was the Battle of Snowshoes, which took place on March 13, 1758. Major Robert Rogers, head of a British ranger company, led a band of nearly two hundred men to scout French positions in the area. William Johnson said of Rogers, "I believe him to be as brave and honest a man as any I have equal knowledge of." The scouting party wore snowshoes to navigate some 4 feet of accumulated snow. Rogers was not happy with the mission, having been given a much smaller force than he requested and believing that the French knew of his plans. He would later say of his orders they "appeared to me . . . incomprehensible." Abenaki scouts discovered the men's tracks, and the French sent a mainly Indian force to confront the rangers. In the fierce battle that ensued, British troops suffered substantial casualties. Scrambling to escape, Rogers threw off his regimental coat and other belongings. Some believed he was killed. A story emerged that he survived by sliding 400 feet down a hillside onto a frozen Lake George. More likely, the Indians halted their pursuit. The spot is still known as Rogers's Rock. He would go on to lead a Loyalist unit during the Revolution.[4]

The day after the Lake George journey, Jefferson wrote his youngest daughter, Mary. Born in 1778, Mary was called "Polly" in childhood and "Maria" as an adult. John Adams declared in 1787, "in my Life I never Saw a more charming Child." Abigail Adams adored her. In 1787, the Adamses received Polly in England when Jefferson, serving as minister to France, called for her to join him and her older sister Patsy. The nine-year-old girl made the voyage in the care of Sally Hemings, then a fourteen-year-old enslaved girl at Monticello. Polly had not wanted to leave Virginia; she had few memories of her father who had been away since 1784. In meeting her, Abigail wrote Jefferson, "She is a child of the quickest sensibility, and the maturest understanding, that I have ever met with for her years." She had less favorable things to say about Sally Hemings, whom she claimed "wants more care than the child and is wholly incapable of looking properly after her, without some superiour to direct her." Abigail opposed slavery (in 1774, she wrote John, "I wish most sincerely there was not a Slave in the province. It allways appeard a most iniquitious Scheme to me–fight ourselfs for what we are daily robbing and plundering from those who have as good a right to freedom as we have"), and her comments about Hemings are not without value, particularly given Jefferson's pending relationship with her. At the same time, they reveal typical attitudes among elite white people about the ungovernability of Black people.[5]

Polly became further agitated when Jefferson did not personally come to meet her. Instead, he sent his maître d', who did not speak English, to bring her to Paris. Abigail told Jefferson, "Tho she says she does not remember you, yet she has been taught to consider you with affection and fondness, and depended upon your comeing for her. She told me this morning, that as she had left all her Friends in virginia to come over the ocean to see you, she did think you would have taken the pains to have come here for her, and not have sent a man whom she cannot understand. I express her own words." If Jefferson was pained, he did not say so. Reunited with her father, Polly attended the same convent school as her sister. Fearful that Patsy wanted to convert to Catholicism, he withdrew them from the school, and in 1789 the family returned to the United States.[6]

Away on his tour with Madison, Jefferson wrote from Lake George to say, "I think always of you." His letters to Maria typically inquired about her ongoing efforts to study and learn. In April 1790, for example, he asked, "Write me a letter by the first post and answer me all these questions. Tell me whether you see the sun rise every day? How many pages a-day you read in Don Quixot? How far you are advanced in him? Whether you repeat a Grammar lesson every day? What else you read? How many hours a day you sew? Whether you have an opportunity of continuing your music? Whether you know how to make a pudding yet, to cut out a beef stake, to sow spinach? Or to set a hen?" Jefferson described himself to her as "a vagrant for a father," and being away compelled him to parent by letter.[7]

Jefferson followed up with peevish missives wondering why Maria had not responded: "I wrote to you three weeks ago, and have not yet received an answer"; "I hope you will now always write immediately on receiving a letter from me"; "I have written you, my dear

60 A JOURNEY NORTH

Maria, four letters since I have been here, and I have received from you only two. You owe me two then, and the present will make three. This is a kind of debt I will not give up." And he didn't give it up. "No letter from you yet, my dear Maria. You now owe me four"; "I did not write to you, my dear Poll, the last week, because I was really angry at receiving no letter. I have now been near nine weeks from home, and have never had a scrip of a pen, when by the regularity of the post, I might receive your letters as frequently and as exactly as if I were at Charlottesville. I ascribed it at first to indolence, but the affection must be weak."[8]

When she did respond, Maria's letters were brief. Jefferson could not have been happy with her report in April 1790 that "I have not been able to read in Don Quixote every day, as I have been travelling ever since I saw you last, and the dictionary is too large to go in the pocket of the chariot, nor have I yet had an opportunity of continuing my music." In February 1791, she wrote, "I am very sorry that my not having wrote to you before made you doubt of my affection" and signed off "Adieu my Dear Papa & believe me to be your affectionate daughter." At one point, she turned the tables: "It is three weeks my Dear Papa since I have had a letter from you. However as it is now my turn I shall not be ceremonious."[9]

Perhaps the thirteen-year-old did not feel much authentic affection for the man she addressed as Papa. Perhaps she knew she could get more attention by not responding than by writing. Perhaps all the questions and admonitions made the teenager roll her eyes. It could not have helped when Jefferson offered such criticisms as "I find I have counted too much on you as a Botanical and zoological correspondent." Whatever her reasons for not responding regularly, Jefferson did not relent and informed her on May 8 that he would not be writing for a few weeks. Rather than head south, he was heading north: "I set out to join Mr. Madison at New York, from whence we shall go up to Albany and Lake-George, then cross over to Bennington and so through Vermont to the Connecticut river, down Connecticut river by Hartford to New-haven, then to New York and Philadelphia." In typical didactic fashion he told her to take out a map and trace the route.[10]

From Lake George, Jefferson found a moment to write on birch bark. Doing so clearly appealed to him because he went through the trouble of drafting the letter on paper and then copying it onto the bark. Maybe he wanted to pique his reader's curiosity (two other personal letters on the trip were also written on birch bark). As a naturalist, he knew the importance of making use of the bark. In his directions to Meriweather Lewis in 1803, he would advise the explorer to make copies of his notes on birch which was "less liable to injury from damp than common paper." Jefferson explained to Mary, "I write to you on the bark of the Paper birch, supposed to be the same used by the antients to write on before the art of making paper was invented, and which being called the Papyrus, gave the name of paper to the new invented substitute."[11]

He went on to say, "I write to you merely to tell you that I am well, and to repeat what I have so often before repeated that I love you dearly, am always thinking of you." If only he had stopped there. Jefferson, however, could not contain himself and went on to advise, "Go on then my dear Maria in your reading, in attention to your music, in learning to manage the kitchen, the dairy, the garden, and other appendages of the household." A month later, he wrote from Philadelphia saying he hoped she had received the letter from Lake George and expected her to give him an account of the geography of the trip when he next saw her. On July 31, he still had not heard back. She had written on July 16 to say that she thought the bark prettier than paper.[12]

Jefferson also wrote his older daughter, Martha, known as "Patsy" when young. Born in 1772, she was six years older than Maria. She had married in 1790 to planter and politician Thomas Mann Randolph and became a mother in 1791 to the first of twelve children, Anne Cary Randolph, making Jefferson a grandfather. (They would name three of their sons Thomas Jefferson Randolph, James Madison Randolph, and Benjamin Franklin Randolph.) The baby had been born in January, and Martha asked her father to name the child; he had not yet done so by March. She expressed a hope of seeing her father during the summer and added, "Your little grand daughter thinks herself entitled to a visit. I hope you will not disappoint us."[13]

Although not as frequently, Jefferson also scolded Martha for not writing and once explained, "Perhaps you think you have nothing to say to me. It is a great deal to say you are all well, or that one has a cold, another a fever &c., besides that there is not a sprig of grass that shoots uninteresting to me." Jefferson knew himself well; everything was of interest.[14]

62 A JOURNEY NORTH

He began his letter of May 31 saying that he had written Maria the day before. He delighted over Lake George: "its waters limpid as chrystal and the mountain sides covered with rich groves of Thuya, silver fir, white pine, Aspen and paper birch down to the water edge, here and there precipices of rock to checquer the scene and save it from monotony. An abundance of speckled trout, salmon trout, bass and other fish with which it is stored, have added to our other amusements the sport of taking them." By comparison, Lake Champlain "is a far less pleasant water. It is muddy, turbulent, and yields little game."[15]

In his journal, Jefferson detailed the dimensions of the lakes, the mountains, and the growth on both sides of the lake, a "thistle in much abundance as to embarrass agriculture in a high degree." He noted that he had not seen any poplars or dogwoods and no fruit trees except some apples and an occasional cherry tree.[16]

He saved for Martha his thoughts about the climate. Weather, as we've seen, obsessed Jefferson. For fifty years, starting in 1776, with some lengthy gaps, he kept a record of the weather arranged in columns for entries on temperature, barometric pressure, and wind direction. He encouraged Madison to do the same, writing him in 1784: "I wish you would keep a diary under the following heads or columns. 1. *day of the month.* 2. thermometer at sunrise. 3. barometer at sunrise. thermom. at 4. P.M. 7. barometer at 4. P.M. 4. direction of wind at sunrise. 8. direction of wind at 4. P.M. 5. the weather viz. rain, snow, fair at sunrise, &c. 9. weather at 4. P.M. 10. shooting or falling of the leaves of trees, of flours, and other remarkeable plants. 11. appearance or disappearance of birds, their emigrations &c. 12. Miscellanea. It will be an amusement to you and may become useful."[17]

Amusement and use. A student of empirical observation, Jefferson thought it fascinating to follow weather patterns. As a plantation owner, he thought its usefulness evident and he wondered as well about regional differences. In 1790, writing from New York during a furious April snowstorm, Jefferson asked his son-in-law to keep a weather diary at Richmond so that the two could compare observations.

In his letter to Martha, he said the trip so far had been "prosperous and pleasant," but complained about the weather. It had been "as sultry hot through the whole as could be found in Carolina or

Georgia. I suspect indeed that the heats of Northern climates may be more powerful than those of Southern ones in proportion as they are shorter. . . . There is as much fever and ague too and other bilious complaints on Lake Champlain as on the swamps of Carolina." However lovely the New York region was, "on the whole I find nothing any where else in point of climate which Virginia need envy to any part of the world. Here they are locked up in ice and snow for six months. Spring and autumn, which make a paradise of our country, are rigorous winter with them, and a Tropical summer breaks on them all at once." Climate, Jefferson proclaimed, contributes to health and happiness, and he was thankful for the accident of birth that made him a Virginian.[18]

Madison, too, kept close track of the weather, and he and Jefferson often exchanged observations about climate. But if he thought about the climate on his journey with Jefferson, he did not say. Unlike Jefferson, Madison wrote no letters during the trip; at least, none have survived. On May 31, the same day Jefferson wrote to Martha, however, Madison began a journal. He would file it in his papers under the title "Notes on tour to Lakes in 1791." He recorded that they had traveled from Ticonderoga to Lake Champlain and beyond Crown Point toward Split Rock. Rough waters and strong head winds forced them to turn back after a day.

Lodged in Ticonderoga, Madison wrote under various headings, including population, land, cultivation, and trade. He noted that while the east side of Lake Champlain was well settled, on the west side houses were "thinly scattered within view from the lake." Still, settlements were rapidly forming. The price of land on the east side was 2 dollars an acre unimproved, and double that if improved. He could not discover the price on the west side. Grass (timothy and red clover) and wheat, he noted, were the staples. An acre of good land yielded 30 bushels of Indian corn rye, potatoes, and flax, but no hemp. Production of maple sugar for domestic use was increasing fast. Wheat went for 50 cents to 2.3 dollars a bushel, and wheat, flour, and pot and pearl ashes were the main exports. He observed that wheat in New York had an advantage over Canada and that "the future & permanent course of the trade will depend much on the improvements that may be made in the communication with the Hudson." He noted that dry goods could be imported more cheaply through Canada than New York because of the duties on them and

64   A JOURNEY NORTH

that smugglers actively brought tobacco, French brandy, and tropical fruits across Lake Champlain into Canada.[19]

The next day, Jefferson and Madison returned to Fort George, and Madison made a noteworthy entry in his journal:

> At Fort George are a few families concerned in the litter trade & ferriage thro the Lake. On the East side not a House is seen except one at the North end owned & inhabited by a free Negro. He possesses a good farm of about 250 Acres which he cultivates with 6 white hirelings for which he is said to have paid about 2½ dollrs. per Acre and by his industry & good management turns to good account. He is intelligent; reads writes & understands accounts, and is dextrous in his affairs. During the late war he was employed in the Commissary department. He has no wife, and is said to be disinclined to marriage: nor any woman on his farm. On the West side from Fort George to Sabath day point (24 miles) not a house is seen except a hut near the fort inhabited by the family of a hunter.[20]

This free Black farmer caught Madison's attention. The man owned a house and a farm; he employed six white workers; he exhibited "industry and good management," skills to be admired by any farmer; and he was literate and "dextrous"—adroit, skillful, perhaps even clever. His service in the Revolutionary War merited attention. Madison at this point in his life was also not married; perhaps he related to this man's disinclination for a wife. It is an admiring portrait of someone surprising enough to Madison to merit a long entry in a journal otherwise devoid of people.

The man was Prince Taylor, and perhaps it is telling that Madison did not use his name. Taylor was from Lunenburg, in Worcester County, central Massachusetts. His father was enslaved and he had been born in 1755. Taylor served five months as a steward on the brig *Diligent* in 1779 before being discharged. In 1781, he accepted a bounty to enlist in the Continental Army, the 6th Regiment of the Massachusetts Infantry. He used his skills as a cooper to earn extra pay repairing barrels. Some five thousand Blacks fought in the Continental Army. While there was considerable opposition at first, George Washington and others came to appreciate the necessity of allowing them to serve to counteract British efforts to induce the enslaved to run away and fight for the British. Madison in 1780 had

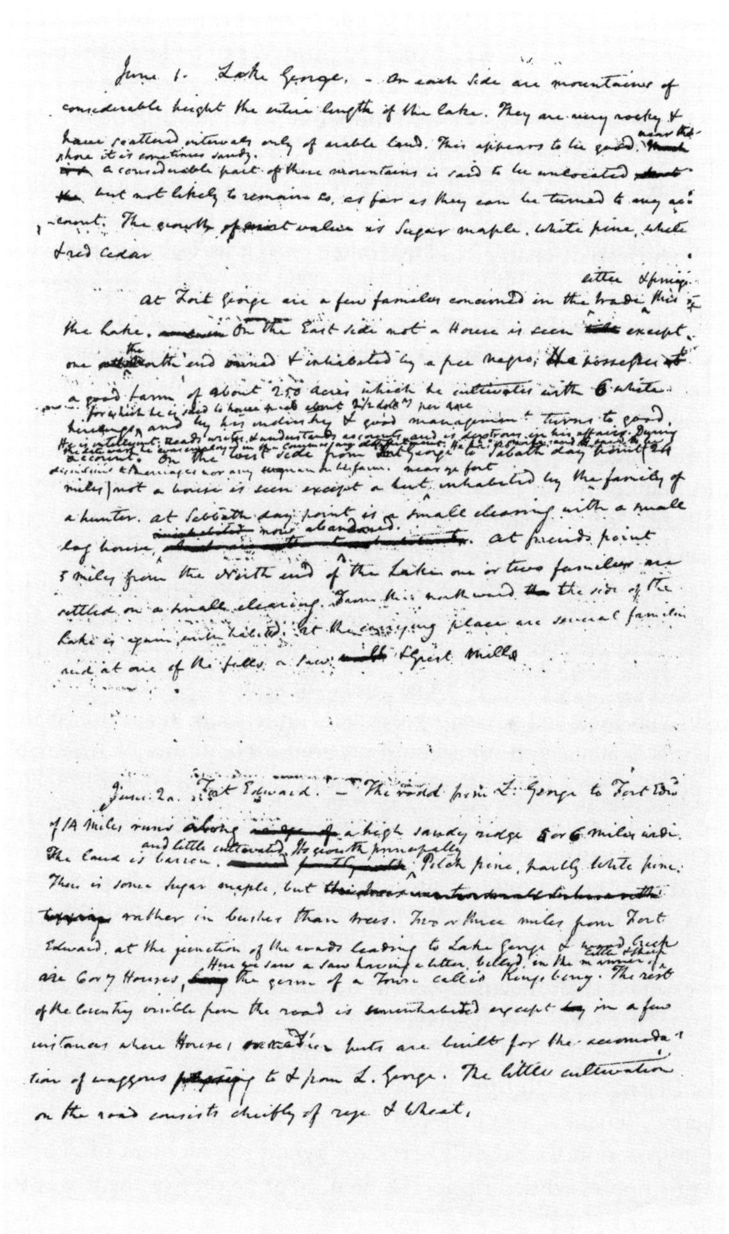

Figure 5 Madison's Journal Entry on Prince Taylor, June 1, 1791 (private collection)

66 A JOURNEY NORTH

noted that enlisting Black men would "certainly be more consonant to the principles of liberty which ought never to be lost sight of in a contest for liberty." He had gone on to say they would pose no danger because they would be outnumbered by whites and their example would not disturb the institution of slavery because "a freedman immediately loses all attachment & sympathy with his former fellow slaves."[21]

Taylor was discharged in December 1783; if he was enslaved when he enlisted, he would have been freed for having served. After the war, he moved to the frontier. He helped a war veteran survey a 500-acre land grant near Lake Champlain and, for his efforts, was given land in payment. In 1791, he purchased a 250-acre farm on a peninsula near Fort Ticonderoga, and he played a prominent role in the community as a founding member of the Episcopal church and helping to survey roads. Other travelers made note of him as well. In 1805, a writer would call Taylor "a free son of Africa" and observe that he held one of the best farms in the area. It is unclear what happened with the farm; perhaps age compelled him to abandon farming. In 1811, he would open an inn and tavern, the first in Ticonderoga. In his pension application in 1818, he declared, "I am by trade a Saylor." A list of assets amounted to 69 dollars and 43 cents and included a cow, two calves, some tools, furniture, plates, utensils, a Bible, and other religious books. He wrote, "I am unable to perform manual Labour by reason of age & two ruptures, which have been of long standing." He received a pension of 8 dollars a month. When he died in 1828, age seventy-three, he was remembered as "a man of wit, of good parts, and withal sincere piety."[22]

We do not know what Madison made of Taylor. In 1785, he had referred to emancipation as "the event which is dreaded." He once proclaimed that his wish was "to depend as little as possible on the labour of slaves." Yet he never figured out how to do so and ultimately surrendered the goal. By the end of his life, he would argue that Blacks were "infinitely worsted by the exchange from slavery to liberty." Jefferson also believed the time had not yet come and precipitous action would only serve to "retard the moment of delivery to this oppressed description of men." For neither of them was the time ever right.[23]

Madison believed emancipation could not occur without colonization and that free Blacks should not live in the United States.

From 1787 to 1788, he had roomed with Quaker physician William Thornton, whose antislavery activities led him to arrange for free Blacks to settle at the mouth of the Sierra Leone River in West Africa. "The blacks who form this settlement," wrote Thornton in the 1780s, "should be a free and independent People, governed by their own Laws, and by officers of their own election." In a letter to a French abolitionist society, he included an insertion from Madison about the establishment of a settlement of free Blacks.[24]

Madison believed that a settlement on the coast of Africa offered "the best hope yet presented of putting an end to the slavery in which not less than 600,000 unhappy negroes are now involved." He thought one of the problems with manumission was that the freedmen retained "the vices and habits of slaves" and placed society at risk. The only way to make manumission safe was if "a compleat incorporation" of slaves into society could be effectuated. This, however, was impossible because of "the prejudices of the Whites, prejudices which proceeding principally from the difference of colour must be considered permanent and insuperable." (Madison never altered his views on white prejudice and the problem of skin color. Thirty years later, as president, he wrote Edward Coles, his private secretary who had left Virginia for Illinois where he freed his slaves, that "I wish your philanthropy would compleat its object, by changing their colour as well as their legal condition. Without this they seem destined to a privation of that moral rank & those social blessings, which give to freedom more than half its value.")[25]

The only solution to the dilemma of freedom and race, thought Madison, was "some proper external receptacle," either the interior of America or the coast of Africa. The problem with settling the American wilderness "a considerable distance from the White frontier" was that the "Savages who have a peculiar antipathy to the blacks" would destroy them, and if too close to white settlements, the same might result. The answer was thus colonization, and Madison thought that if slaveowners knew their freed slaves would leave, it might make them more amenable to manumission.[26]

Thornton added, "such is his Opinion, and he further intimated that Slavery is not likely to be *ever* abolished in the Southern States of America till an Asylum be provided to which the manumitted Blacks may be sent." Madison never changed his mind. To the end of his life, he would insist "the freed blacks ought to be permanently

68   A JOURNEY NORTH

removed beyond the region occupied by or allotted to a White population," and he served as president of the American Colonization Society from 1833 until his death.[27]

Whatever Madison thought about the fate of emancipated Blacks, his personal experience illustrates the complexities that underlie slavery and freedom. In 1783, at the conclusion of the fighting in the American Revolution, Madison had written from Philadelphia to his father about Billey, an enslaved young man who was born in 1759. Under the Pennsylvania Gradual Abolition Act of 1780, resident slaveowners had to register their property, and nonresidents could not keep their slaves in the state longer than six months. Madison's situation with Billey was different, and he told his father, "I have judged it most prudent not to force Billey back to Va. even if could be done; and have accordingly taken measures for his final separation from me." Madison concluded, "I am persuaded his mind is too thoroughly tainted to be a fit companion for fellow slaves in Virga. . . . I do not expect to get near the worth of him; but cannot think of punishing him by transportation merely for coveting that liberty for which we have paid the price of so much blood, and have proclaimed so often to be the right, & worthy the pursuit, of every human being."[28]

It is a profound statement, recognizing how the principles of the Revolution spread and acknowledging Billey as a thinker. (Many enslaved persons made the connection: in 1777, "a Great number of Blackes" petitioned the Massachusetts legislature for their "Natural and Inalienable right" of freedom.) Of course, Madison had also been concerned with not losing money. Rather than free him outright, he sold Billey as an indentured servant with a term of seven years. Billey began using his full name, William Gardner. Madison remained in contact with him and, in 1787, inquired if he knew anything about a runaway named Anthony. Gardner worked at a boarding house and as a merchant seaman and agent. In 1793, Madison, who was in Montpelier, would ask Gardner to keep an eye out for a vessel arriving with a plow he had ordered. Jefferson agreed to pay Gardner on Madison's behalf (34.70 dollars). Jefferson also employed Gardner's wife, Henrietta, to do laundry. In January 1791, he had written in his account book, "Billy's wife (Mrs Gardener) begins to wash for me at £20. a year." She continued to do so while Jefferson was secretary of state and again as vice president. Sometimes Gardner collected the laundry payment from Jefferson. William Gardner would meet a sad end in 1795 when, on a voyage to New Orleans, he took ill and fell overboard.[29]

It is hard, however, not to wonder what James Hemings thought of men such as William Gardner and Prince Taylor. Hemings was, of course, an accomplished chef. In Paris he earned wages, and in France he could have petitioned for his freedom. But he did not. He also remained in Philadelphia for longer than six months at a time. Perhaps he was standing by some agreement he made with Jefferson in Paris to return with his sister Sally to Monticello. Perhaps it took time for the examples of free Black men living as they chose to germinate. Whatever the tipping point, in 1793, Hemings made that deal with Jefferson for his freedom and was finally emancipated on February 5, 1796.

Like Madison, Jefferson believed in colonization. In the aftermath of a Virginia slave conspiracy in 1800, the president would correspond with Governor James Monroe about likely destinations for slaves suspected of "conspiracy, insurgency, treason, rebellion" and suggested the West Indies, where "Nature seems to have formed these islands to become the receptacle of the blacks transplanted into this hemisphere." The following year he settled on Africa as "the most desireable receptacle." Emigration, he said, must be annexed to emancipation. He continued both as president and private citizen to solicit locations for colonization. In 1814, he told Edward Coles, "I have seen no proposition so expedient on the whole, as that of emancipation of those born after a given day, and of their education and expatriation at a proper age."[30]

Jefferson also thought the problem of race insurmountable, though for different reasons than Madison, for whom color was not necessarily a bar to moral and social uplift; rather, it presented a problem mainly because of white reactions to racial differences. By comparison, Jefferson ascribed innate defects to Blacks. He told Coles, "this color we know, brought up from their infancy without necessity for thought or forecast, are by their habits rendered as incapable as children of taking care of themselves." In his *Notes on the State of Virginia*, first published in 1785, Jefferson had written about "the real distinctions which nature has made" between whites and Blacks and noted that "the first difference which strikes us is that of colour." Jefferson proceeds to offer a breathless condemnation of the Black race that even in its own time might have been seen as extreme. The color black offered "eternal monotony." Blacks were ruled by sensation, not reason. They had no imagination. They sweat less and were more ardent. He concluded that they were "inferior to the whites in the endowments both of body and mind. . . .The unfortunate differences of colour, and perhaps of faculty, is a powerful obstacle to the emancipation of these people. . . . The slave, when freed, he is to be removed beyond the reach of mixture."[31]

What did Jefferson think of Prince Taylor and William Gardner and other freed Blacks? How is it that this man of the Enlightenment who valued experience did not modify his views when faced with the example of Black men who succeeded as free men? He fathered at least six children with Sally Hemings, four of whom lived to adulthood and were the only enslaved persons he emancipated. One of them, born in 1805, he named James Madison Hemings. Were they eligible for freedom only because he was their father or because Sally Hemings, their mother, demanded it as a condition of her ongoing servitude?

In August 1791, only weeks after the northern journey, a free Black man confronted Jefferson on his racial beliefs. Maryland-born Benjamin Banneker had largely taught himself math, surveying, and astronomy. He prepared an almanac for publication and decided to send Jefferson a handwritten copy. With it, he enclosed a long letter. It is telling that the 1,400-word missive does not begin, as one might expect, with Banneker informing the secretary of state that he is enclosing a copy of the almanac. That comes only toward the end. Rather, he begins by telling Jefferson, "I suppose it is a truth too well attested to you, to need a proof here, that we are a race of Beings who have long laboured under the abuse and censure of the world, that we have long been looked upon with an eye of contempt, and that we have long been considered rather as brutish than human, and Scarcely capable of mental endowments."[32]

Banneker proceeds to challenge Jefferson's racial assumptions and hold him to the truths of the Declaration of Independence: "Sir how pitiable is it to reflect, that altho you were so fully convinced of the benevolence of the Father of mankind, and of his equal and impartial distribution of those rights and privileges which he had conferred upon them, that you should at the Same time counteract his mercies, in detaining by fraud and violence so numerous a part of my brethren under groaning captivity and cruel oppression, that you should at the Same time be found guilty of that most criminal act, which you professedly detested in others, with respect to yourselves."

Saying that he "freely and Chearfully" acknowledges that "I am of the African race and, and in that colour which is natural to them of the deepest dye," he informs Jefferson it is his "indispensable duty" to exert his "power and influence" to liberate Blacks from prejudice and oppression. Only then does he mention the almanac, handwritten, not printed, so that Jefferson "might view it in my own hand writing," the implication being that, otherwise, Jefferson might not believe it was his work.

Jefferson responded ten days later. He thanked Banneker for the Almanac and assured him, "No body wishes more than I do to see such proofs as you exhibit, that nature has given to our black brethren, talents equal to those of the other colours of men, and that the appearance of a want of them is owing merely to the degraded condition of their existence both in Africa and America." He told Banneker he would send the ephemeris to Condorcet, the French philosopher and mathematician who was secretary of the Royal Academy of Science in Paris. This he did, and in his cover letter to Condorcet Jefferson seemed enthusiastic about Banneker, whom he called "a very respectable mathematician." "I shall be delighted to see these instances of moral eminence so multiplied as to prove that the want of talents observed in them is merely the effect of their degraded condition, and not proceeding from any difference in the structure of the parts on which intellect depends."[33]

However, no amount of proof was enough for Jefferson to make the leap from perceiving the effects of slavery to endorsing its abolition. By 1809, he revised his opinion of Banneker, writing to Joel Barlow that he has "a mind of very common stature" and thought his work was aided by the surveyor Andrew Ellicott, whose family belonged to the Maryland Society for the Abolition of Slavery. Jefferson no longer thought the topic of "the grade of understanding of the negroes," as he wrote in another letter, worthy of much attention.[34]

Jefferson surrendered to his prejudices and gave up. When Edward Coles wrote in July 1814 to inform him of his decision to free his slaves and move to Illinois, he implored Jefferson to use his influence to promote a plan of emancipation. Given his "professed and

72 A JOURNEY NORTH

practiced" principles of liberty, believed Coles, the "duty . . . devolves particularly on you."[35]

Jefferson responded that while he believed "the hour of emancipation is advancing," the work ahead was not for his generation. "This enterprise is for the young, for those who can follow it up, and bear it through to its consummation, it shall have all my prayers." Coles retorted that he did not agree prayers were all Jefferson had to offer. He reminded Jefferson that at the end of his life another luminary, Ben Franklin, had been "actively and usefully employed" in opposing slavery. Coles had the last word.[36]

Madison, too, was asked to act. Among the letters written to him while he was away with Jefferson on the northern journey was one from Robert Pleasants, a Virginian and a Quaker who founded the Virginia Society for Promoting the Abolition of Slavery in 1790. Pleasants wrote to ask if Madison would bring a petition against the international slave trade before the House and asked for his opinion on petitioning the Virginia General Assembly for an act that would allow masters to free the children of slaves when they reached a certain age. Pleasants was jumping ahead; manumission had only become legal in Virginia in 1782. "[S]eeing we live in an enlightened age, when liberty is alowed to be the unalianable right of all mankind," he wrote Madison, "it surely behoves us of the present generation, and more especially the Legislature, to endeavour to restore one of the most valuable blessings of life, to an injured and unhappy race of people."[37]

Madison's response no doubt disappointed the abolitionist. As to the petition against the slave trade, he would not "become a volunteer in giving a public wound, as they would deem it, to an interest on which they set so great a value." Whatever Madison might have thought, his constituents came first. As for petitioning the General Assembly, he believed it might lead to repeal of the law giving masters discretion to free their slaves, or perhaps lead to an amendment requiring freed slaves to leave Virginia. Basically, Madison thought it best not to confront lawmakers with such inflammatory issues for fear that it would do more harm than good.[38]

Four decades later, Edward Coles, who had already failed with Jefferson, challenged Madison directly. He implored Madison to make provisions in his will to free his slaves. "It seems to me repugnant to the distinctive and characteristic traits of your character—nay

AT FORT GEORGE: PRINCE TAYLOR (JUNE I)

pardon me for saying, it would be a blot and stigma on your otherwise spotless escutcheon, not to restore to your slaves that liberty and those rights which you have been through life so zealous & able a champion." He noted that if Jefferson, who had died a few years earlier, had failed to do so, that was because he was in debt. Madison's finances were more secure, he thought, and he had no children to provide for. As for Mrs. Madison, the manumissions could be staggered to make certain that she had the care she needed. Emancipation was always attended with difficulties, but the problems were temporary. Freedom was permanent. Freeing your slaves in your will, Coles admonished Madison, "is absolutely necessary to put a proper finish to your life and character." Madison did not respond.[39]

In retirement, Madison came to lament slavery as "the great evil under which the nation labors" and "a sad blot on our free country." That was the easy part. The hard part was doing something about it. Madison had by this point many examples of former slaves now freed who lived among whites, worked diligently, and enjoyed their liberty. Although he took notice of them, he never abandoned his belief in colonization, never overcame his prejudice against race, and never set his slaves free.

Departing Fort George during that northern journey, Madison thought no further about Prince Taylor, a free Black who had fought in the Revolution, owned a productive farm, and enjoyed the fruits of his freedom.[40]

At Bennington: Sugar Maple (June 4–5)

On June 3, Jefferson and Madison crossed the Hudson at Saratoga, on their way to Vermont. They had breakfast that morning at McNeal's, which Jefferson rated as "middling." They had passed through Fort Edward, and Madison noted that the landscape was "barren, and little cultivated." The growth was principally pine, though Madison noticed some sugar maple. It was not a casual observation: both men had become interested in the domestic production of maple sugar. Jefferson paid .125 dollars to have his horses reshod. The men paused to witness a sow having a litter.[1]

Madison made an extensive entry in his journal. He noted that the distance from Saratoga to Bennington was 31 miles. He commented upon the topography, several miles of pine barren followed by miles of "hilly clayey and middling land" strewn with sugar maple and white pines and the more mountainous ground. A fertile vale separated two ridges of low mountains. Outside the pine barrens, the land was densely settled. Madison noted that in addition to "Wheat rye Some Indian Corn potatoes & flax & potash . . . some sugar is made & much may be. The attention seemed to be increasing toward that object." Madison reported that while in New York land was held both by lease (at 1/8 dollar per acre) and fee-simple (outright ownership), farms in Vermont, ranging from 50 to 200 acres, were owned "wholly in fee." The settlers in Vermont were emigrants from Massachusetts and Connecticut, and their "living is extremely plain & economical," particularly in furnishings and dress. The houses, made of wood, impressed Madison, who thought "they make a good figure without."[2]

AT BENNINGTON: SUGAR MAPLE (JUNE 4–5)   75

Vermont loomed large in Jefferson's and Madison's thinking, and one reason for this northern journey was to visit the newly admitted state. In 1777, Vermont had declared itself an independent republic and adopted a constitution that echoed the Declaration of Independence, providing for freedom of religion and banning slavery. Any discussion of Vermont becoming the fourteenth state had to await the resolution of New York's competing land claims. Sometime after 1784, Madison expressed his satisfaction that the conflict would be decided by judicial means, by the "empire of reason," and not by the sword. A few years earlier, he predicted that Vermont would become a "separate & federal State" in a "train of speedy decision." That "speedy decision" would take ten years.[3]

Jefferson, for one, was worried about what he called the "Vermont doctrine" whereby "the Vermonteers insist that on the demolition of the regal government all the municipal laws became abrogated." Such a pernicious doctrine threatened "the dissolution of the social contract on a revolution of government." He worried, in 1783, that the Virginia assembly was drifting in this same direction and feared "the pride of independance [sic] taking deep and dangerous hold on the hearts of individual states." Only by strengthening the connecting band through Congress could dissolution be prevented.[4]

The ratification of the Constitution certainly strengthened the federal government, yet it did little to entice the Vermont republic. Ethan Allen, who had led the so-called Green Mountain Boys during the Revolution, opposed New York over the land grants that would become Vermont. He had flirted with Quebec about making Vermont a British province, and he thought the states would fail to unite under a new government because "they are spread over different climates, have different religions, prejudices, customs, and interests." Influential as he was, Allen did not control Vermont politics, and the drift toward joining the United States accelerated, hastened no doubt by Allen's death in 1789.[5]

The path toward statehood was cleared when New York and Vermont resolved their territorial dispute. In January 1791, Vermont authorized payment of 30,000 dollars to New York to terminate the land claims and was now free to seek admission to the Union. On February 7, George Washington met with Nathaniel Chipman and Lewis Morris, commissioners from Vermont chosen to present

76   A JOURNEY NORTH

a memorial for admission. (The meeting was delayed two hours because President Washington was out riding his horse for his health.)

On February 9, Washington informed the Senate that he had received from Governor Thomas Chittenden documents that confirmed New York's consent that Vermont should be admitted "to be a distinct member of our Union." In their memorial to the president and Congress, Chipman and Morris testified that the citizens of Vermont "having shared in common with those of the other states, in the hazards and burthens of establishing the American revolution, have long anxiously desired to be united with them, under the same general government."[6]

Chipman, a Yale graduate and chief judge of the Vermont Supreme Court, played a pivotal role in the republic's shift toward statehood. He knew nothing could be done unless those land claims with New York were settled and in 1788 had solicited Alexander Hamilton's help to resolve them. He told Hamilton, "the people of this State, should certain obstacles be removed, I believe, might be induced almost unanimously, to throw themselves into the Federal state." Hamilton responded enthusiastically. He pointed out that Vermont's admission would be particularly welcome because deliberations over admitting Kentucky were about to begin and the "Northern [states] will be glad to send a counterpoise in Vermont." Hamilton would play a role in the final compact between New York and Vermont, and he no doubt advised Chipman on how best to appeal to the president and Congress for admission—by mirroring the language of Kentucky's petition, which praised the new Constitution and pledged attachment to the Union.[7]

As a prerequisite to admission, Vermont ratified the Constitution on January 10, 1788 (by a vote of 105–4). Instrumental to the ratification was Robert Morris, who also signed the memorial to the president. Morris had served as an aide to Philip Schuyler and George Clinton during the Revolution and moved to Vermont in 1786. A prominent businessman, he held a variety of political offices and served as clerk of the Vermont House of Representatives and a member of the Vermont Constitutional Convention. Washington would appoint him the first U.S. marshal of Vermont, and he would eventually be elected to the House of Representatives. Chipman would serve on the United States District Court and as a senator from Vermont. On February 18, 1791, Washington signed the bill that would admit Vermont as the fourteenth state. (Kentucky would follow the next year.)

Jefferson and Madison came to Vermont to see the natural landscape and also to gauge the political climate. The *Vermont Gazette* noted their arrival and applauded the statesmen for "acquainting themselves with the state of population, situation and extent of the empire to which their abilities are devoted." By traveling through the region, "they obtain a personal knowledge of the abilities and prejudices of the citizens of different parts, and find the surest mode of reconciling differences."[8]

Anthony Haswell, the editor of the newspaper, had arrived in Bennington from Massachusetts, where he had served his apprenticeship and edited several newspapers. His politics ran Republican, and as an editor he did not shy away from controversy: he printed Ethan Allen's deist tract *Reason, the Only Oracle of Man*, a pamphlet condemned by Christians who saw it as a sign from heaven when a print-shop fire, caused by lightning, destroyed most copies. In time, Haswell's Jeffersonian principles would lead him to be arrested and convicted of seditious libel.

A week after Jefferson and Madison had departed, Haswell was still thinking about them and reported that "they expressed great satisfaction with the country through which they had passed on their tour." Haswell described the travelers as affable and polite and noted that they won over "the sentiments of the people, and secured to themselves a fund of political knowledge, which cannot fail to render them more essentially serviceable to their country." Jefferson must have appreciated meeting Haswell—in August, a contingent expense of the Department of State was a subscription to the *Vermont Gazette*.[9]

Madison and Jefferson met the editor at the home of former Governor Moses Robinson, who hosted them for the weekend. They began their stay at Robinson's mansion overlooking the Walloomsac River and then retreated to his farm because of the heat. Robinson had helped navigate Vermont's path toward statehood, and he would soon be elected to the United States Senate.

Joining Robinson and Haswell was Joseph Fay, who had fought in the Battle of Bennington during the Revolution and served as Vermont's secretary of state between 1778 and 1781. All three men gravitated toward anti-Federalism and settled comfortably into

78   A JOURNEY NORTH

Democratic-Republican politics, though in a conversation with Jefferson and Madison about Paine's recently published *Rights of Man*, Fay defended the British government. A few months later, he wrote Jefferson to retract his earlier opinion, confessing that Paine "has in a *Masterly* Manner pointed out the defects of British Government, and plainly shewn that they have no Constitution, and reflected great light to the world relative to the Natural rights of Man."[10]

Some of the political knowledge gained by Jefferson and Madison concerned relations with Canada and the status of British outposts in the region. After the Revolution, the British maintained posts at Point au Fer, in New York, and Dutchman's Point on North Hero Island, inside Vermont territory. Vermonters became incensed over the presence of a British ship that stopped boats passing to and from Canada to assess custom-house duties. Jefferson wrote to Washington on June 5 to share what he had discovered about reports that "something disagreeable had taken place in the vicinities of the British posts." What he learned was that the ship's "exercise of power further within our jurisdiction became the subject of notice & clamour with our citizens in that quarter." The British, for their part, were alarmed by plans for the creation of a custom-house at Alburgh, opposite Point au Fer. Jefferson wrote that "a groundless story of 200 Americans seen in arms near Point au fer, has been the cause, or the pretext, of their reinforcing that place a few days ago with a company of men from St John's." Those concerns persisted, and the following year Jefferson heard from the British minister at Philadelphia about acts of violence being committed in Alburgh, where residents loyal to Great Britain were being forced to leave. Jefferson assured the British minister that he would investigate, and he wrote to Governor Chittenden, who simply ignored the secretary of state.[11]

While in Vermont Jefferson also inquired about what was taking place with the Canadian government. He reported to Washington that there was division between English and French residents over the preferred forms of government, "the English who desire something like an English constitution but so modelled as to oblige the French to chuse a certain proportion of English representatives, & the French who wish a continuance of the French laws, moderated by some engraftments from the English code." The Constitutional Act of 1791, passed by Parliament a few days after Jefferson's letter,

AT BENNINGTON: SUGAR MAPLE (JUNE 4–5)   79

divided the territory into Lower and Upper Canada and went into effect at year's end.[12]

Part of what necessitated the change was the thousands of loyalists who fled to Canada following the Revolution. The events of the Revolutionary War, which had ended only a few years earlier, were never far from Jefferson's and Madison's thoughts as they visited some of the notable battlefield sites of the war. Jefferson wrote his son-in-law on June 5 that he and Madison had toured "the principal scenes of Burgoyne's misfortunes, to wit the grounds at Still water where the action of that name was fought and particularly the breastworks which cost so much blood to both parties, the encampments at Saratoga and ground where the British piled their arms, and the field of the battle of Bennington, about 9 miles from this place." They also visited Forts William Henry, George, Ticonderoga, and Crown Point, all of "which have been scenes of blood from a very early part of our history."[13]

On May 28, they toured several sites of the Battle of Saratoga. In July 1777, British General John Burgoyne had captured Fort Ticonderoga and Fort Edward. American General Philip Schuyler retreated to Stillwater and was relieved of command, replaced by Horatio Gates. Burgoyne attacked at Freeman's Farm on September 19 and then at Bemis Heights on October 7 (the first and second Battles of Saratoga). Ten days later, Burgoyne surrendered. Jefferson and Madison were accompanied by John Schuyler, whose father, Philip, asked him to escort them "over the grounds . . . by the British and American armies previous to the surrender of the latter and point out the ground on which the British piled their arms."[14]

The victory led the French to recognize the United States. In the aftermath, Samuel Chase, who would one day serve on the Supreme Court (and whom Thomas Jefferson sought to have impeached), proclaimed in 1778, "America has now taken her rank among the Nations & has it in her power to secure her Liberty & Independence." By the time of their visit, Saratoga had already been enshrined as central to the story of American national identity. David Ramsay, in *The History of the American Revolution*, published in 1789, proclaimed that Burgoyne's surrender at Saratoga "vibrated round the world" and was "the hinge on which the revolution turned."[15]

The battlefield in 1791 still had visible fortifications, entrenchments, and graves. Duc Rochefoucauld, who visited the battle

80   A JOURNEY NORTH

grounds in 1795, called them a "truly *memorable* place, which may be considered as the spot where the independence of America was sealed." He reported that the spot of the surrender "remains exactly as it then was," except for the regrowth of bushes that had been cut down by the two armies. By the first decades of the nineteenth century, development had largely erased the signs of battle. One writer lamented in 1821, "few vestiges are to be seen; the plow has strove with insidious zeal to destroy even these few remaining evidences of Revolutionary heroism." Not until the centennial of 1877, when the cornerstone of the Saratoga monument was laid, did efforts to preserve the battlefield materialize.[16]

On June 4, Jefferson and Madison toured the grounds of the Battle of Bennington, a key victory in the prelude to the triumph at Saratoga, fought on August 16, 1777. The hero of the battle was John Stark, who organized the militia to oppose Burgoyne's approaching force. Stark had led a New Hampshire regiment at the battles of Trenton and Princeton in 1776 but resigned his commission when passed over for promotion. Recognizing the threat posed by a British invasion from Canada, Stark began assembling a force, and the New Hampshire Provincial Congress commissioned him a brigadier general to lead the men. Burgoyne sent a force to Bennington in search of supplies. The detachment, which consisted of German, British, loyalist, and Indian combatants, encountered Stark and his men. Legend has it that before attacking he inspired his men by exhorting that "Tonight the American flag floats from yonder hill, or Molly Stark sleeps a widow!" Burgoyne's force was soundly defeated, and the battle stood as a momentous precursor to what was yet to come. George Washington wrote on August 22, "I hope the whole Force of that Country will turn out, and by following the great stroke struck by Genl Stark near Bennington intirely crush Genl Burgoine." Stark eventually received the promotion he had earlier been denied when Congress advanced him to major general in 1783. When he died at age ninety-four in 1822, he was the last surviving American-born Revolutionary War general.[17]

Though neither Jefferson nor Madison met with Stark during their visit, in time, as presidents, they both wrote to Stark to acknowledge his service. Jefferson learned in 1805 that the general was still alive and noted that "the victories of Bennington, the first link in that chain of successes which issued in the surrender at Saratoga, are still

AT BENNINGTON: SUGAR MAPLE (JUNE 4-5)   81

fresh in the memory of every American, & the name of him who achieved them dear to his heart." Four years later, in 1810, Madison wrote to Stark to acknowledge "the part you bore as a Hero and a Patriot, in establishing the Independence of our country" and congratulate the hero of Bennington on "the opportunity which a protracted life has given you of witnessing the triumph of republican Institutions so dear to you." Stark used his response as an occasion to warn Madison about the British: "If the enmity of this British nation is to be feared, their alliance is much more dangerous. For I have fought with them and against them and I found them treacherous and ungenerous as friends, and dishonourable as enemies." Two years later, there would again be war with the British.[18]

Jefferson and Madison were not the first to visit these battlefields as memorial sites and cause for celebration. In July 1783, months before the Treaty of Paris was signed, Washington decided he wanted to tour the northern parts of New York "to reconnoitre those places where the most remarkable Posts were established, and the ground which became famous by being the theatre of Action in 1777." He visited Lake George, Fort Ticonderoga, and Saratoga. The traveling party, which included Alexander Hamilton, lodged with Phillip Schuyler. Whatever Washington thought of the battlefields, he was taken by the springs at Saratoga and even sought to purchase them— he failed in the endeavor. He did, however, manage to obtain 6,000 acres of adjoining territory in the Mohawk Valley. Washington turned a nice profit on the land, which cost him 1,875 pounds. He sold parts of it ten years later for 6,000 pounds.[19]

Jefferson and Madison could not leave Bennington on June 4 because the next day was Sunday, and Vermont laws prohibited travel on the Sabbath. On the morning of the fifth, they took breakfast at Elijah Dewey's inn, which dated from 1771 and had been the scene of many Vermont political meetings during the Revolutionary era. Dewey had been a captain in the Bennington militia and fought in the area's battles. Jefferson rated the inn as "good." Following breakfast, they met with Governor Robinson, who brought his guests to services at the First Congregational Church. It is hard to know what they thought of the excursion. Jefferson was famously a deist whose religious views led the Federalists to denounce him as a heretic and infidel. Madison, more circumspect than Jefferson in expressing his

82 A JOURNEY NORTH

personal religious beliefs, fought vigorously for religious liberty and played a key role in the passage of Jefferson's Bill for Establishing Religious Freedom, approved by the Virginia Legislature in 1786. One story circulated that Robinson, extremely pious and proud of the choir, asked his guests what they thought of the singing, to which they replied they could not judge as they had not been to church for some time.

The Reverend Job Swift was in the pulpit and delivered that day's sermon. He was an ally of Timothy Dwight, an orthodox Congregationalist who, as president of Yale from 1795 to 1817, waged a vigorous campaign against what he called "infidel philosophy." He dedicated himself to defeating the Jeffersonians, whom he described as "the illuminati, the philosophers, the atheists, and the deists." Swift graduated from Yale in 1765 and took the pulpit in Bennington in 1786. His son recalled that as a minister of the Gospel his father felt compelled "to resist the flood of infidelity and licentiousness that threatened to sweep away the foundations of all civil, social, and religious institutions." When Jefferson became president, Swift refused to pray for him in the weekly litany. The increasingly Republican Bennington would force the Federalist preacher to leave the congregation in 1801.[20]

Swift was not a charismatic orator. He would dutifully pick a biblical passage and explicate it along orthodox doctrinal lines. We do not know what sermon he preached on June 5. Whatever the topic, Jefferson, in particular, must have been bemused. Jefferson rejected the Trinity, Jesus's divinity, original sin, and miracles, among other Christian doctrines. While professing to believe in God, he rejected all denominations. "I am of a sect by myself, as far as I know," he proclaimed.[21]

Robinson later took the occasion of Jefferson's election to the presidency in 1800 to write a congratulatory letter. He informed Jefferson that the hostility toward Republicans, who "were Represented as Enemies to their Country and friends to France," had subsided, though the eastern part of Vermont continued to be hostile to the Jeffersonians. Jefferson responded that because of the "dominion of the clergy, who had got a smell of union between church & state," the eastern parts would be the last to come over. He no doubt was aware of comments such as that from one New England newspaper prior to his election: "Should the infidel Jefferson be elected to the

AT BENNINGTON: SUGAR MAPLE (JUNE 4–5)   83

Presidency the *seal of death* is that moment set on our holy religion, our churches will be prostrated, and some infamous prostitute, under the title of the Goddess of Reason, will preside."[22]

Jefferson replied to Robinson that he thought the clergy would eventually come around. They would "find their interest in acquiescing in the liberty & science of their country, and that the Christian religion when divested of the rags in which they have inveloped it, and brought to the original purity & simplicity of it's benevolent institutor, is a religion of all others most friendly to liberty, science, & the freest expansions of the human mind."[23]

Following services on June 5, Jefferson wrote his letters to Washington and Randolph. He told Washington that the next day they would head into the Green Mountains, though with their cavalry in part disabled, he was unsure about their progress. He explained to Randolph that they had covered about 400 miles in their journey and had about 450 miles to go. He also gave Randolph a full botanical report on the plants and objects that pleased him:

> Those either unknown or rare in Virginia were the Sugar maple in vast abundance, the Thuya, silver fir, White Pine, Pitch pine, Spruce pine, a shrub with decumbent stems which they call Junaper, an Azalea very different from the Nudiflora, with very large clusters of flowers, more thickly set on the branches, of a deeper red and high pink-fragrance. It is the richest shrub I have seen: the honey suckle of the gardens growing wild on the banks of Lake George, the paper birch, an Aspen with a velvet leaf, a shrub willow with downy catkins, a wild gooseberry, the wild cherry with the single fruit (not the bunch cherry), strawberries in abundance.[24]

Jefferson loved botany and ranked it with "the most valuable sciences." It was the underpinning of his interests in gardening and agriculture and his identity as a naturalist. He obsessed over plants, collecting as many as he could. As minister to France, he would have plants from North America shipped to him so he could impress the Europeans with their size and beauty. He also sought seeds of plants and trees for the garden of Madame de Tesse, a countess and prominent salon leader who returned the favor—in 1809, she sent Jefferson seeds of a Chinese goldenrain tree. "I cherish it with particular attentions," he wrote, "as it daily reminds me of the friendship

84 A JOURNEY NORTH

with which you have honored me." In 1812, he provided an extensive list of cuttings and seeds to Bernard McMahon, Philadelphia nurseryman and author of *The American Gardener's Calendar* (which Jefferson purchased in March 1808 for 3 dollars and 50 cents) to "add a little to my former wants so as to put me in possession once and for all of every thing to which my views extend, & which I do not now possess." He also sent McMahon some seeds which he thought the nurseryman did not have. Jefferson must have been thrilled when, at a meeting of the American Philosophical Society in 1792, Benjamin Barton Smith announced that a newly discovered wildflower would be named *Jeffersonia*.[25]

It is not surprising that in his letter to Randolph Jefferson he listed the sugar maple first. Madison also featured it in his journal: "The sugar maple White Oak, Beach & sometimes white pine make the principal figures in its forests." Their interest in the sugar maple was not merely anecdotal or aesthetic. Several Revolutionary leaders had come to see the production of maple sugar as a boon to domestic production and as a way to reduce reliance on sugar cane as a sweetener. This would allow the United States to decrease its dependence on imports from British traders. The cultivation of the sugar maple, some hoped, might also serve to accelerate the end of slavery in the West Indies.[26]

Earliest references to the sugar from the maple tree date to the seventeenth century. Sometimes it was called "maple water," and missionaries and colonists learned the art of making it from Native Americans. In 1705, Robert Beverly noted, "The Sugar-Tree yields a kind of Sap or Juice, which by boiling is made into Sugar. This Juice is drawn out, by wounding the Trunk of the Tree, and placing a Receiver under the Wound." The English had only known of it for a decade or so, yet "it has been known among the Indians longer than any now living can remember."[27]

Colonists may not have thought much about sugar before Parliament passed the Sugar Act in 1764 and maintained a high tax on imported sugar (among other provisions that concerned molasses and rum). Benjamin Franklin, however, saw the consequences and noted that "great quantities" of sugar could be made from the sugar maple. Little came of the suggestion then. In the 1780s, however, a fellow Philadelphian would help launch a sugar maple craze.[28]

Figure 6 Sugar Maple Tree (Library of Congress))

86   A JOURNEY NORTH

Benjamin Rush was among the early advocates of the sugar maple. Leading physician, signer of the Declaration, friend to Jefferson and Adams, Rush wrote essays on various subjects, including education, religion, punishment, and Indians, not to mention health, both physical and mental. In 1788, he published an essay on "Advantages of the Culture of the Sugar Maple Tree" in which he provided directions on how to make maple sugar (tap trees in February, strain, boil, skim, and granulate). He concluded that a farmer, in winter no less, "could raise nothing on his farm with less labour." The following year, Rush helped found the Society for Promoting the Manufacture of Sugar from the Sugar Maple. In August 1789, he met several Quaker merchants and philanthropists and proposed that the newly formed organization purchase 500 barrels of maple sugar every year "to lessen or destroy the consumption of West India sugar, and thus indirectly to destroy negro slavery."[29]

Rush was not alone in this view. Brissot de Warville, who founded a French abolitionist society, Society of the Friends of the Blacks, toured the United States in 1788 and later wrote, "on this continent . . . so polluted and tormented with slavery, Providence has placed two powerful and infallible means of destroying this evil. The means are the societies of which we have been speaking, and the sugar maple."[30]

In the decades before Rush expressed his concerns about slavery and sugar, Quakers such as John Woolman and Benjamin Lay advocated a sugar boycott. In his journal for 1769–1770, Woolman wrote that he had seen the oppression of the enslaved and, "wanting to live in the spirit of peace and minister no just cause of offense to my fellow citizens . . . I have for some years past declined to gratify my palate with those sugars."[31]

Rush's awakening to the problem of cane sugar occurred at the same time as an abstinence campaign in Great Britain was taking hold. The Society for the Abolition of the Slave Trade, founded in 1787, gathered petitions signed by hundreds of thousands. In 1791, when Parliament failed to pass a bill abolishing the slave trade, abolitionists pressed for a boycott of slave-grown sugar. William Fox, an abolitionist bookseller, wrote *An Address to the People of Great Britain, on the Utility of Refraining from the Use of West India Sugar* (the title changed over various editions). More than 200,000 copies circulated widely in Great Britain and America. Fox thundered

AT BENNINGTON: SUGAR MAPLE (JUNE 4–5)

against slaveholders and traders and drew the connection to consumers: "whatever we do by another, we do ourselves." "So necessarily connected are our consumption of the commodity, and the misery resulting from it," he calculated that "in every pound of sugar used . . . we may be considered in consuming two ounces of human flesh." Several hundred thousand Britons participated in the boycott.[32]

Rush, a member of the Pennsylvania Abolition Society, relied less on moral appeals than on practical ones to persuade others of the desirability of the sugar maple. He conducted an experiment to show that the strength of the sugar maple was not inferior to West Indian cane sugar. He served tea prepared with both sugars to a group that included Alexander Hamilton and Henry Drinker, and reported that they could not discern a difference. Drinker, a successful Quaker merchant, was so taken with the idea of maple sugar production, he had his agent cultivate sugar on his Delaware estate and in 1790 send a sample to George Washington, who replied that he was pleased to find it of such good quality and was persuaded that it was a promising industry that would benefit the country.[33]

Tench Coxe was also charmed by the idea. A political economist and assistant secretary of the treasury under Hamilton, Coxe loved statistics (he would provide the charts and tables for Hamilton's *Report on Manufactures*). In 1790, he noted that in Pennsylvania small quantities of maple sugar were being produced in large part because of their "great and increasing dislike of Negro slavery." Coxe crunched the numbers to prove that domestic production of maple sugar could replace imports of cane sugar, which exceeded 8 million pounds a year. William Cooper, lawyer and landholder, founder of Cooperstown, started a maple sugar business in 1789 and informed Coxe that 5 pounds of sugar could be made from a tree, and there were forty trees to an acre. Coxe therefore calculated that some 52,000 acres would yield the amount needed to replace imports— and that there was significantly more of that acreage available. A few years later, he raised his estimates, yet the conclusion remained: a family could produce maple sugar as easily as soap, cheese, or beer. Another writer agreed: "a man, aided by four children, may easily, during four weeks of running of the sap, make fifteen hundred pounds of sugar."[34]

In March 1790, Rush met with Jefferson, who was on his way to New York to serve as secretary of state. Rush described him as "plain in his dress and unchanged in his manners." Rush's proselytizing clearly had an impact. In June, Jefferson informed Benjamin Vaughan that "late difficulties in the sugar trade have excited attention to our sugar trees," a reference to the elimination of sugar imports from British colonies after the Revolution. The United States, he argued, was covered with sugar maple trees, and sugar from the tree was every bit as good as Caribbean cane sugar. Moreover, the trees, if skillfully tapped, would last for years. Not the least, "What a blessing to substitute a sugar which requires only the labour of children, for that which it is said renders the slavery of the blacks necessary." In November, Jefferson purchased 50 pounds of refined maple sugar. Madison, too, became aware of the possibilities. In notes for a speech in Congress in May 1790, he wrote "sugar can be got from Maple trees."[35]

Before leaving on his journey, Jefferson informed Thomas Mann Randolph that "evidence grows upon us that the U.S. may not only supply themselves the sugar for their own consumption but be great exporters." He said the same to William Drayton, president of the South Carolina Agricultural Society. He also informed George Washington that Arthur Noble, William Cooper's partner in the maple sugar business, had visited and provided "flattering calculations" about the value of the product. Jefferson was especially excited to learn from Noble that it was less profitable to convert the tree's juice into spirits than sugar, though he noted that a sample tasted exactly like whiskey. Jefferson told Noble that "in a few years we shall be able to Supply half the World." By July 1791, Rush claimed that "Mr. Jefferson uses no other sugar in his family than that which is obtained from the sugar maple tree."[36]

On May 13, 1791, Henry Drinker had breakfast with Jefferson. Afterward, he wrote to a friend that Jefferson and Madison were about to set off on a tour through "an extensive Sugar Maple country." While the sugar maple may not have been as explicit an objective as the Hessian fly, it captured Jefferson's attention. In his journal on May 27, he wrote simply, "Cohoes. Sugar Maple." From Bennington, he informed his son-in-law that he was "pleased with the botanical objects which presented themselves," especially the sugar maple, which was "rare or unknown in Virginia." Among the

AT BENNINGTON: SUGAR MAPLE (JUNE 4–5)   89

topics discussed in Bennington at dinner with Robinson, Fay, and Haswell was the sugar maple. Haswell wrote in the *Vermont Gazette*, "it is reported from good authority" (Jefferson, no doubt) "that there are maples in the inhabited parts of the United States, more than sufficient, with careful attention, to produce sugar adequate to the consumption of its inhabitants," and that "attention to our sugar orchards is essentially necessary to secure the independence of our country."[37]

Sugar maple trees were not the only way Jefferson sought to reduce reliance on imports from the West Indies. A few weeks earlier, at the town of Hudson, he met with Captain Seth Jenkins, a whaler who founded the town's port in 1783 and ran a distillery that exported a thousand hogsheads (each held over 60 gallons) of rum per year. Over breakfast, Jefferson tried to persuade him to use wine rather than imported molasses to manufacture the spirits. The suggestion perhaps had the added benefit of expanding trade with France. George Beckwith, a British agent, thought this the purpose of the whole northern trip: "to feel the pulse of the country and to advocate his favorite objects in behalf of France." Whatever Jefferson's intent, he failed to persuade Jenkins, who wrote Jefferson in July that the wines of Southern France "cannot answer for Distilling in this Country."[38]

Whatever his hopes for wine, Jefferson never lost his enthusiasm for sugar maples. At trip's end, on June 15, he visited William Prince's nursery in Flushing. Established in the 1730s, it was America's first commercial nursery and by the 1790s offered every variety of tree, advertising some ten thousand and countless plants. Madison had first told Jefferson about Prince in 1787. He called him a "man of worth . . . who has been generally very successful in preserving the trees from perishing by such distant transplantations," and enclosed a catalog. Only later in the same letter did he mention that "The Constitution proposed by the late Convention engrosses almost the whole political attention of America."[39]

Jefferson was enthralled by the nursery, though George Washington, who visited in 1789, wrote that "it did not answer my expectations." Jefferson, ever the collector, left a note for Prince that listed the trees that he wanted to order. At the top of the list, "Sugar maples, all you have." (He also included cranberries, poplars, sumacs, pears, plumbs, nectarines, peaches, apples, and roses.)[40]

Figure 7 Catalog of Prince Nursery, 1771 (Special Collections, Oregon State University)

AT BENNINGTON: SUGAR MAPLE (JUNE 4–5) 91

Jefferson's first attempt to grow sugar maples had begun the previous year. On December 16, 1790, he sent Randolph sugar maple seeds as well as pecan nuts with instructions to "make George prepare a nursery in a proper place" and plant the seeds. George was George Granger, Sr., a slave whom Jefferson had purchased in 1773 and who was put in charge of what Jefferson described as "my orchards, grasses &c." In time, he served as an overseer. The verb "make" stands out. Not "ask" or "tell" or "instruct."[41]

Before leaving on the northern trip, Jefferson had asked Randolph how well the sugar maple planting had succeeded. He learned from Randolph shortly after his return that "The Sugar maple has failed entirely, a few plants only having appeared which perished almost immediately." Jefferson responded that he had taken measures to procure a new supply of seeds and had purchased trees from Prince's nursery. Those trees, sixty of them, arrived in Richmond in December. That planting also did not succeed. Randolph remarked how delicate the tree was. Jefferson, however, was not to be deterred. "I am sorry to hear my sugar maples have failed," he wrote in April 1792. "I shall be able however to get here any number I may desire, as two nurserymen have promised to make provision for me. It is too hopeful an object to be abandoned."[42]

In his ongoing quest for sugar maples, Jefferson did not rely solely on Prince's nursery. On July 2, more than a year after the trip, he wrote to a friend, "I am now endeavoring to procure as many as I can of the Sugar maple trees, to commence large plantations of these." A few days later, he wrote Madison that he saw advertised for sale in New York grained maple sugar and asked if he could acquire 100 pounds and ship it to Richmond, from where it would be forwarded to Monticello. He added, "I presume on your having got over your indisposition; if not, I beg you to let all this matter rest till you are." Madison replied that his health had improved. Unfortunately, the manufacturers of the sugar Jefferson saw advertised would not sell in parcels less than 1,500 pounds and only at auction. He managed to procure another sample of maple sugar, but thought it of inferior quality. Jefferson wrote Hugh Rose that it did not answer his purpose.[43]

Jefferson also procured seeds from Joseph Fay. He wrote in August to thank him for considering his request and added, "Every thing seems to tend towards drawing the value of that tree into public notice. The rise in the price of West India sugars, short crops, new embarrasments which may arise in the way of our getting them, will oblige us to try to do without them." In November, Fay wrote, "I am sorry to inform you that not a single seed of the Maple has come to maturity this year in all this Northern Country." Fay noted the high price of imported sugar was due in part to "the insurrection in the Islands," a reference to the slave revolt in Saint-Domingue that had begun on August 21, 1791. The domestic maple sugar business was more important than ever.[44]

In November 1791, Jefferson wrote William Short, his former private secretary, "Such is the avidity for Maple sugar, that it is engaged in the country before it comes to market. I have not been able this year to buy a pound for myself." He noted, "there is no doubt but that were there hands enough in the Sugarmaple country, there are trees enough not only to supply the U.S. but to carry a great deal to Europe and undersell that of the cane. The reason why it may be cheaper, is that it is the work of women and children only, in a domestic way, and at a season when they can do nothing in the farm. The public attention is very much excited towards it."[45]

Finally, in October 1792, Fay forwarded maple seeds to Jefferson and asked that he offer some to Madison, as well as a small bunch he enclosed for Washington. Jefferson did so. It was not the first time the president received maple sugar seeds. On August 7, 1791, Washington examined a sample from Arthur Noble and William Cooper, who informed him "that a Sufficient quantity of this Sugar may be made in A few years to Suply the whole United States." Washington forwarded the seeds to Mt. Vernon and told his estate manager, "Let the Gardener put all the Seeds of the Sugar Maple in the ground this Fall; but not to cover them more than very slightly indeed, with Earth." Washington had as little success as Jefferson in growing the trees.[46]

On August 19, 1791, at the height of the maple sugar frenzy and shortly before the rebellion in Saint-Domingue, Benjamin Rush delivered an address to the American Philosophical Society. It took the form of a letter to Jefferson, and it would be published separately the following year as *An Account of the Sugar Maple-Tree of the United States*. Rush introduced the sugar maple to his audience, which included Jefferson and Benjamin Smith Barton, physician and professor of natural history and botany at the College of Philadelphia.

AT BENNINGTON: SUGAR MAPLE (JUNE 4–5) 93

Rush explained that thirty to fifty trees grow per acre and that a tree yields 20 to 30 gallons of sap, from which 5 or 6 pounds of sugar can be made. The more frequently the tree is tapped, the more syrup is obtained. Tapping best occurs on mild days and cold nights in February through March.

Rush then explained the methods for reducing sap to sugar (freezing, evaporation, and boiling) and refining it into loaf sugar. Rush compared the quality of maple sugar to cane sugar from the West Indies and proclaimed it was better because it was purer and just as strong. It was also cheaper to produce. He marveled at the resources in America for producing maple sugar. He calculated that 60,000 families could produce 135 million pounds of sugar (three persons per family with each tending 150 trees that produce 5 pounds per tree). He put domestic consumption at 120 million pounds, which would leave 15 million pounds for export. Dr. Rush also promoted the benefits of sugar in one's diet, arguing that it offered nourishment and prevented disease and malignant fever (although diabetes has been known since antiquity, not until the late nineteenth century was the disease more fully understood). Rush added, "it has been said that sugar injures the teeth, but this opinion now has so few advocates that it does not deserve a serious refutation."[47]

The sugar maple should be embraced because of its profitability (Rush calculated that each farmer would yield an annual profit of 80 dollars) and because of humanity: "I have persuaded myself to behold in it the happy means of rendering the commerce and slavery of our African brethren in the sugar islands as unnecessary as it has always been inhuman and unjust."[48]

Whatever the humanitarian impulses, commercial sugar maple production did not deliver on its promise. Henry Drinker went into business with William Cooper and provided kettles so that settlers in Otsego could harvest sap. The results, however, were disappointing (Cooper shipped only one-fifth the amount expected in 1790). In 1792, the same year that the Society for the Promotion of Useful Arts in New York published a letter from Cooper that waxed enthusiastic about the sugar maple, he told Drinker that he was quitting the trade. Drinker, Rush, and Coxe were among the many subscribers who had committed to paying 7 pence per pound for sugar Cooper would deliver, and they all lost their investments. Drinker's own enterprise, Union Farm, failed in 1794. Rush sold the lands

94 A JOURNEY NORTH

associated with the Society for Promoting the Manufacture of Sugar from the Sugar Maple Tree.[49]

Foreigners, too, sought to invest. The Holland Land Company sent John Lincklaen as one of its agents to explore the territory. He carried with him a letter of introduction from Alexander Hamilton, who wrote William Cooper in August 1791 that Lincklaen was traveling to explore "what can be done with regard to the manufacture of the Maple Sugar." Lincklaen and a colleague began their travels in August 1791 and covered over 2,000 miles through Pennsylvania, New York, Vermont, and Connecticut. In Vermont, Lincklaen wrote that he decided to travel on the Sabbath though he risked being arrested. He commented that while there was a considerable number of maple trees, "the people do not seem to me to be persuaded of the advantages they might gain from this tree." The problems with sugar maple production in Vermont were numerous: too much snow, no home market, and excessive cost of transportation. In the end, the Holland Land Company purchased several million acres of land in western New York. Within two years, they closed their maple sugar operation outside of Utica.[50]

Not until later in the nineteenth century would Vermont come to be identified as the preeminent producer of maple sugar and syrup. By then, cane sugar had taken hold in Louisiana, where the enslaved population quadrupled and planters provided a quarter of the world's supply. Talk of domestic maple sugar production as a means to combat slavery vanished.[51]

Whatever his reasons (dismay over West Indian slavery, a desire to reduce imports from British merchants, the ideal of the self-sufficient family farm, botanical exuberance), Jefferson remained steadfast in his enthusiasm for the sugar maple and never abandoned his quest to grow a maple orchard in Monticello. In 1808, he exclaimed, "I have never seen a reason why every farmer should not have a sugar orchard, as well as an apple orchard." The following year he wrote, "I propose to make me a large orchard of Paccan & Roanoke & Missouri scaly barks which I possess, & of Gloucester & common scaly barks of which I shall plant the nuts. to these I shall add the sugar maple tree if I can procure it. I do not see why we may not have our sugar orchards."[52]

At Poospatuck: Unkechaug Indians (June 14)

On June 6, before sunrise, Jefferson and Madison left Bennington. Jefferson again had his horse shod, and the men took breakfast at Killock's Inn in Williamstown. That evening they lodged in the town of Dalton at Marsh's, the town's leading public house. Madison described the valley through which they passed in the 38 miles they covered that day as "rich level & well cultivated." He thought it "pretty closely settled" with small New England farms. The forests were predominantly sugar maple, white oak, and beech, and in the fields he saw wheat, rye, oats, Indian corn potatoes, and flax. All the trade, he noted, went down the Connecticut River to New York.[1]

The next day, they made their way across the foothills of the Berkshires to the Connecticut River and arrived in Northampton. Madison noted that while the west side of the mountains allowed for the cultivation of wheat, the east side "is so liable to be blasted as to be little sown." Despite the disadvantages of a more severe climate on the eastern side because of the winds, the area was well settled, "in some places very thickly." Wooded land sold for 3–6 dollars per acre; improved land for 5–6 dollars. The trade, Madison noted, flowed to Springfield and Hartford. June 7 was Madison's final entry in his journal. Jefferson's was on June 3, though he kept up his inquiries into the Hessian fly and his ratings of inns and distances traveled. Perhaps the men were tiring of their trip. Perhaps what lie ahead, Hartford and Long Island, then back to Brooklyn and New Yok, was familiar enough not to warrant comment.[2]

Though they were entering a political hotbed of Federalism and Anti-Federalism, they said nothing in writing about it. At Northampton, they lodged at Pomeroy's Red Tavern (which

96   A JOURNEY NORTH

Jefferson rated as "good"). The tavern was apparently a meeting place for Anti-Federalists, those who had opposed ratification of the Constitution. No state was as divided over ratification as Massachusetts, which became the sixth state to do so with a vote of 187–168 on February 6, 1788. In general, the eastern parts of the state supported the Constitution whereas western Massachusetts was opposed, but it varied from town to town. Northampton voted to ratify. Nearby West Springfield voted against, while East Springfield voted for.

If any of the tensions surrounding ratification of the Constitution and Bill of Rights drew Jefferson's and Madison's attention during their stay, they left no record of it. Jefferson crossed the Connecticut River to East Springfield, not to probe political differences, but to view up close two large elms that he had spotted. He later lamented to Madison that they did not collect samples of leaves, "as it is the leaf which principally decides *specific* differences." He then re-crossed and the men headed to Hartford, where they spent two nights at Frederick Bull's coffee house, which Jefferson rated as "good" (he had stayed there once before).[3]

Hartford was a center of New England Federalism. Connecticut had ratified the Constitution by a vote of 128–40, and Federalists represented the state until the party itself collapsed after a convention in Hartford in 1814 that decreed opposition to the War of 1812. Perhaps given the city's Federalism, Jefferson and Madison opted simply to pass the days quietly (the second night was occasioned because Madison's horse became lame). If they met with any political leaders, there is no record of it.

Though Madison and Jefferson said nothing about the Federalists, the Federalists disparaged the visit of the Republican statesmen. In a long, gossipy letter, Nathaniel Hazard, a New York merchant, informed Alexander Hamilton of what he had heard at a dinner in Hartford attended by Federalist luminaries, such as Governor Samuel Huntington, Oliver Wolcott, William Johnson, and John Trumbull. At the dinner, Pierpont Edwards, a prominent politician and lawyer, "ridiculed, J——n & M——n's Tour; in which they scouted silently thro' the Country, shunning the Gentry, communing with & pitying the Shayites, & quarrelling with the Eatables; nothing good enough for them." He thought the poet John Trumbull would write a "stinging satire" about the tour.[4]

AT POOSPATUCK: UNKECHAUG INDIANS (JUNE 14) 97

The comment reflects the Federalists' antipathy toward Jefferson and Madison and their paranoia over the tour. To these diners, Jefferson and Madison were Shaysite—referring, of course, to Shays's Rebellion—sympathizers quietly scouting the area for Democratic-Republican supporters. Some Federalists had convinced themselves that the statesmen sought to bring down Hamilton. In his *History of the Republic of the United States*, published decades later, John C. Hamilton, Alexander Hamilton's son, proclaimed that the entire trip was intended to sow opposition to his father "under the pretext of a botanical excursion."[5]

Jefferson and Madison opposed Hamilton; that was clear to all. There is no reason, however, to believe that they desired to advance support for republican policies in Hartford. More likely, they were happy simply to pass the time there and move on to the final leg of their journey.

How different it had been for Jefferson seven years earlier when he passed through the city. Named minister plenipotentiary to France in 1784, he traveled across Connecticut, Rhode Island, New Hampshire, and Massachusetts on his way to Boston to sail for Europe. His oldest daughter, Martha, and James Hemings accompanied him. Along the way he gathered information about agriculture, commerce, and geography to help inform him in his new role. He met with several leading politicians, including Governor Jonathan Trumbull of Connecticut and Governor Jabez Brown of Rhode Island as well as Governor John Hancock of Massachusetts.

At New Haven, he stopped to visit Ezra Stiles, the president of Yale. They shared wide-ranging interests in science and natural history (Stiles had corresponded with Benjamin Franklin in the 1750s on those subjects), and a few days later, writing from Hartford, Jefferson began a correspondence with him on the size of mammals in North America. After Jefferson departed, Stiles described him in his diary as "a most ingenious Naturalist & Philosopher—a truly scientific & learned Man—& every way excellent."[6]

Jefferson returned from France in 1789 to learn of his appointment as secretary of state. Writing from Paris, he expressed "hope to receive soon permission to visit America this summer, and to possess myself anew, by conversation with my countrymen, of their spirit and their ideas. I know only the Americans of the year 1784. They tell me this is to be much a stranger to those of 1789." Part of

98   A JOURNEY NORTH

his northern tour with Madison was to have such conversation with countrymen.[7]

The two moved on from Hartford to Middletown. Jefferson had, as noted, stopped writing in his journal, yet he made one last undated entry. He marveled over a wheel to draw water and, in typical fashion, measured the diameter and axis and observed, "the weight descends to the ground outside of the well when the bucket is drawn up, and when you send down the bucket you wind up the weight." Jefferson loved machines and technology. He invented a wheel cipher, owned multiple polygraph machines for copying letters, and installed dumbwaiters at Monticello. Although concerned initially about monopolies, he came to support the first Patent Act, passed in 1790. Indeed, as secretary of state, he was responsible for administering patent requests, an obligation he found burdensome. (In 1802, Madison, as secretary of state, created a separate patent office.) On its passage, Jefferson described the Patent Act as having "given a spring to invention beyond my conception."[8]

On June 11, the two boarded a sloop and crossed Long Island Sound to Oysterpond Point. The 40-mile overnight voyage must have terrified Madison, who had a deep fear of sea travel; it was likely the longest of his life. Before departing, Jefferson had expressed to members of the American Philosophical Society that he was keen to visit Long Island because the area had been ravaged by the Hessian fly.

They spent the next two days traveling across Long Island, to Riverhead and Moriches, where they lodged at Downs tavern, which Jefferson rated as "good." The next morning, the men traveled 7 miles to Mastic, the estate of William Floyd. They had breakfast with Floyd, whom they knew well. Jefferson refers to him in one place as "Colonel" and another as "General." Floyd had been in the Suffolk County militia during the Revolution and served as a delegate to the Continental and Confederation Congress. He was a signer of the Declaration of Independence and had recently completed a term in the first session of the House of Representatives. For a time in 1783, Madison, Jefferson, and Floyd resided at the same boardinghouse in Philadelphia.

Visiting Floyd must have been uncomfortable for Madison. In 1783, he had—as briefly recounted earlier—courted Floyd's fifteen-year-old daughter Catherine "Kitty" Floyd. Age thirty-two, Madison was not the most adroit in social situations. The teenager

AT POOSPATUCK: UNKECHAUG INDIANS (JUNE 14)   99

charmed him, and she was flattered by his attention. Jefferson wrote to Madison to say he noticed the flirting and hoped there was something to it. Madison responded, "your inference on that subject was not groundless. Before you left us I had sufficiently entertained her sentiments." The two exchanged miniature portraits painted by Charles Wilson Peale and became engaged. When the Floyds left Philadelphia for New York on April 29, Madison accompanied them as far as New Brunswick, New Jersey.[9]

The joy Madison felt in the spring turned to sorrow in the summer. He wrote to Jefferson of his "disappointment" over "the uncertain state into which the object I was then pursuing had been brought by one of those incidents to which such affairs are liable." It was a delicate way of saying that the engagement was off and that Kitty loved another, a medical student whom she would later marry. The sting never fully dissipated. Decades later, Madison would recover his letter to Jefferson and excise in pen what he had written in cipher; it would be over a decade before Madison would marry the twenty-six-year-old widow Dolley Payne Todd in 1794.[10]

Whatever feelings Madison experienced at Floyd's estate, he kept them to himself. As he had throughout the trip, Jefferson posed questions about the Hessian fly. They discussed wind direction and the flight of the fly, which, Floyd thought, traveled 20 miles a year from west to east, yet drifted slowly westward because of prevailing winds. The fly had arrived in 1785, but there were none that year.

After breakfast, Floyd accompanied Jefferson and Madison to the settlement at Poospatuck, where some twenty Unkechaug Indians lived. The Unkechaug are among the Algonquin peoples who had settled the area thousands of years earlier. With colonization, they gradually lost much of their land and adapted to a new economic system in which many worked for colonial estate holders such as Nicoll Floyd, William's father. In the early eighteenth century, a permanent reservation at Poospatuck was established. Its size, however, was consistently whittled down. In 1789, William Floyd persuaded eight Unkechaug to sell him 15 acres at below market price, and he continued to seek rights to the remaining 50-acre reservation.[11]

Jefferson must have been excited by the unexpected opportunity to visit the reservation. His lifelong interest in Native American history and language led him in 1779 to propose an amended constitution for the College of William and Mary whereby professors would appoint qualified missionaries to "the several tribes of Indians, whose business shall be to investigate their laws, customs, religions, traditions, and more particularly their languages, constructing grammars thereof, as well as may be, and copious vocabularies."[12]

Jefferson always admired Indians, confiding to John Adams in 1812 that from an early age he "acquired impressions of attachment & commiseration for them which have never been obliterated." He referred to them as "another edition of man" and believed them to be "in body and mind, equal to the whiteman." (He added that he believed the Black man not to be so.) "We, like you," he told Jean Baptiste Ducoigne, chief of the Kaskasia of Illinois country, "are Americans, born in the same land, and having the same interests." He expressed his curiosity about the paintings on buffalo skins that the tribe gave as a gift and enjoyed smoking the peace pipe, which he called "a good old custom handed down by your ancestors, and as such I respect and join in it with reverence."[13]

Jefferson was not always so benevolent. During the Revolution, he had called them "savages" whose "rule of warfare . . . is an indiscriminate butchery of men women and children." In 1780, he told George Rogers Clark, who led vicious campaigns in Kentucky, Illinois, and Ohio, "the end proposed should be their extermination, or their removal beyond the lakes or Illinois river. The same world will scarcely do for them and us."[14]

The only way the same world might do for both was if the Indians gave up their ways and became civilized. As president, Jefferson accelerated policies begun under Washington. He sought treaties with tribes to secure peace and acquire land. He advocated farming and domestic manufacture over hunting and fishing as a way of life. "What a brilliant aspect is offered to your future history, if you give up war and hunting," he exclaimed in 1808. Various trade and intercourse acts "sought to promote civilization among the friendly Indian tribes." Such policies, Jefferson noted, would also allow Indians to live on smaller portions of land, thus making land acquisition easier for the government to effectuate. Indians, President Jefferson counseled, needed "to place their interests under the patronage of the United States."[15]

In the 1780s, Jefferson's evolving views of Indians were critical to his ongoing attempt to refute the theory of New World degeneracy advocated by Comte Georges-Louis de Buffon in his *Natural*

AT POOSPATUCK: UNKECHAUG INDIANS (JUNE 14)   101

History: General and Particular. Buffon thought the New World inferior to the old and believed America was a land that could "afford nourishment only to cold men and feeble animals." Buffon applied his theory to Indians as well as animals, arguing that they were weak and dull and even claiming they had withered genitalia. Jefferson devoted himself to proving Buffon wrong.[16]

He did so in *Notes on the State of Virginia,* begun in 1781 and expanded and published in a small French edition in 1785. The first American edition appeared in 1788. The book emerged as a comprehensive response to a questionnaire sent in 1780 by Francois Barbe-Marbois, the secretary to the French Legation in Philadelphia, who sought detailed information about each state. Jefferson gladly took on the responsibility of answering for Virginia. The work encompassed much more than a response to Buffon, as Jefferson wrote about various topics, including geography, botany, population, commerce, and laws. He mentioned or cited Buffon nearly two dozen times and included charts comparing European and American quadrupeds to refute the notion that New World animals were smaller than those found in the Old World. Comparisons of the beaver, otter, and shrew mice alone, he showed, offer a correction to Buffon's observation that animals in America are smaller than in Europe.[17]

Madison, too, got caught up in the enterprise of refuting Buffon. He took extensive notes on Buffon's *Natural History* and made his own observations about marmots and moles. He thoroughly examined a weasel and sent Jefferson a chart comparing it with measurements offered by Buffon. Madison said the weasel came into his hands already dead. After examining the length, height, spleen, kidneys, heart, and tongue, as well as teeth and ribs, he concluded that his findings contradicted Buffon's assertion.[18]

If much of Jefferson's observations in the query titled "Productions mineral, vegetable, and animal" were characterized by a dry recital of measurements, he found poetry in the numbers. Buffon's claim that nature could be "less energetic on one side of the globe than she is on the other" appalled him: "As if both sides were not warmed by the same genial sun; as if a soil of the same chemical composition, was less capable of elaboration into animal nutriment; as if the fruits and grains from that soil and sun, yielded a less rich chyle. . . . The truth is, that a Pigmy and a Patagonian, a Mouse and a Mammoth, derive their dimensions from the same nutritive juices."[19]

Jefferson begins his discussion of Indians in Query VI by noting that "hitherto I have considered this hypothesis as applied to brute animals only, and not in its extension to the man of America, whether aboriginal or transplanted." Jefferson challenged aspects of Buffon's characterization of Indians as being feeble and lacking ardor. He saw them as brave ("endures torturers with a firmness almost unknown to religious enthusiasm"), affectionate, and faithful. He noted "the circumstances of their having never submitted themselves to any laws, any coercive power, any shadow of government." He admired them for being governed entirely by their moral sense and speculated that it might be better to live under no law than too much of it. With respect to their "genius," a word Jefferson used repeatedly in discussing cultural achievements, he thought more facts were required and circumstances needed to be considered. He praised Chief Logan's speech to Lord Dunmore in 1774 as an example of Indian eloquence. Referring to himself in the third person, the Chief said, "I appeal to any white man to say, if ever he entered Logan's cabin hungry and I gave him not meat; if ever he came cold or naked and I gave him not clothing." Jefferson thought Europe had not provided a more eminent orator, whether Demosthenes or Cicero.[20]

In Query XI, "Aborigines," he describes at length his excavation of an Indian burial mound. Jefferson wanted to understand Indian burial practices, and to satisfy his curiosity, he dug through the mound and the collection of Indian bones buried below. The skulls were decayed, and they broke apart upon being touched. He noted the remains of children as well and thought that, in all, there were as many as one thousand skeletons. He recalled thirty years earlier seeing a party of Indians proceed directly to the mound and stand with expressions of sorrow by its side. It is likely that Jefferson conducted the dig in 1783, and his analysis of the mound's strata has earned him the title "Father of American Archaeology." In his pursuit of knowledge, however, little was sacred to Jefferson; he gave no thought to the site's desecration.

In the Query, Jefferson discusses the various Indian tribes in Virginia—their origins, population, location, and history. He was especially interested in their languages, because such knowledge might provide evidence of origins. He laments that so many tribes had disappeared without any record of their languages. Jefferson exclaims, "were vocabularies formed of all the languages spoken in

North and South America," studying them would help "construct the best evidence of the derivation of this part of the human race."[21] The origins of Native Americans preoccupied Jefferson. Did they begin in Asia and emigrate to North America, perhaps across the Bering Strait, or through Iceland and Greenland? Perhaps it was the other way around: the Indians originated in North America and migrated to Asia. Language, he believed, held the key. Where there was greater diversity from a common language, there was a greater passage of time. Such was his conclusion in a letter from Paris to Ezra Stiles in 1786. "Among the red inhabitants of Asia there are but a few languages radically different," he wrote. "But among our Indians the number of languages is infinite which are so radically different as to exhibit at present no appearance of their having been derived from a common source." The time needed to generate so many languages must have been immense, he thought. In 1786, he informed Benjamin Hawkins, an Indian agent, "I shall proceed however in my endeavors particularly with respect to their language and shall take care so to dispose of what I collect thereon as that it shall not be lost." The following year he reasserted, "I am persuaded that the only method of investigating the filiation of the Indian nations is by that of their languages."[22]

Jefferson began collecting: Hawkins forwarded a vocabulary of Cherokee and Choctaw words, and Madison sent a pamphlet on the Mohican language. Jefferson thanked his friend and explained, "I endeavor to collect all the vocabularies I can of the American Indians, as of those of Asia, persuaded that if they ever had a common parentage it will appear in their languages."[23]

Jefferson was not alone in his interest in Indian vocabularies. Catherine the Great of Russia sought Indian words for the creation of a universal dictionary of all languages. In 1786, Marquis de Lafayette transmitted the request to George Washington, who replied he would do his best but cautioned that Her Majesty must be patient. Washington wrote various officials, and, the following year, he received from Richard Butler, superintendent of Indian Affairs for the northern district, a Shawnee and Delaware word list. He also received from Madison, who had learned of Catherine's project, the Cherokee and Choctaw vocabulary that Hawkins had sent to Jefferson. Washington forwarded both lists to Lafayette and

104   A JOURNEY NORTH

expressed how gratified he would be if the efforts contributed to
"promoting the affinity of nations."[24]

The excursion to the Unkechaug on June 14 afforded Jefferson the
opportunity to create his own list of Indian words. He noted there
were about twenty members of the tribe and that only three could
still speak the language, a dialect different from two neighboring
tribes in Southampton—in fact so different that they could barely
understand one another. He spoke with two elderly women and
a younger woman who was familiar with the language. He asked
for the Unkechaug equivalent of some two hundred words that he
dictated, drawing on the work that he had begun to accumulate.
Having not expected this opportunity, Jefferson wrote the list in
the blank spaces of an envelope addressed to him that he had in his
pocket. It was the only dialect he ever recorded. (Jefferson spelled
the tribe's name "Unquachog.") He noted "there remain but three
persons of this tribe now who can speak its language."

It is unclear how the list of 201—to be exact—words came to be.
It features some categories: quadrupeds, birds, insects, and plants,
taxonomies that came easily to Jefferson: cow, horse, sheep; bird,
crow, gull; snake, bug, worm; tree, pine, oak. The list moves to
people—woman, child, boy (but not man), body parts, and relations.
Then come some verbs in infinitive form: to run, to break, to kill,
which seem to have inspired the words "war" and "peace." A few
personal pronouns followed by numbers conclude the first column.
The second column includes common farm animals, weather, colors,
and some opposites: good/bad; handsome/ugly; stand/sit. There are
words perhaps related to traditional Unkechaug endeavors: whale,
whale oil, oyster, clam. Wampum, moccasins, and tomahawk are
also on the list. It continues with more numbers and a few theolog-
ical concepts: God, a great God, devil. The list ends with thunder
and lightning.

After his return to Philadelphia, Jefferson created a printed form,
consisting of a list of 282 words that he sent to correspondents, who
would conduct interviews with various tribes to advance the vocabulary project. Vocabulary lists were a burgeoning genre in an age
that sought to collect and categorize human experience. Jefferson
later had in his library Peter Simon Pallas, *Linguarum totius orbis vocab-
ularia comparativa* (1786, though Jefferson did not know of the work

Figure 8 Vocabulary of the Unquachog Indians (American Philosophical Society)

until 1806), Weeden Butler, *The Indian Vocabulary to Which Is Prefixed the Forms of Impeachments* (1788), and Jonathan Edwards, *Observations on the Language of the Muhhekaneew Indians* (1788), among other titles. In 1809, Jefferson noted that his list of 282 words had 73 in common with Pallas's list of 130 words. Those in common included words for things found in nature: fire, water, earth, eye, mouth, blood.[25]

Eighty words on the Unkechaug list did not make it into Jefferson's general form, some for reasons that are understandable: those tied to the whaling industry, for example. Also eliminated were words tied specifically to Native American society, such as wampum and tomahawk. It added numerous words, however, including verbs such as to love, to hate, to see, to smell, to laugh, and to cry. Jefferson sought universality—that alone would lead him to humanity's linguistic origins.

At the end of the Unkechaug list, Jefferson noted "the orthography is English," by which he meant phonetic spelling was used to recreate the sounds. In 1800, the vocabulary project well established, he explained to David Campbell, a judge in Tennessee tasked with completing a list of Cherokee words, "I think it would be best to use the English orthography, only, where there are sounds which that is incapable of expressing." Jefferson ended the Unkechaug formal list by certifying, "This Vocabulary was taken by Th: J. June 13. 1791 in presence of James Madison and Genl. Floyd." The scientific record was important to him. Ironically, he got the date wrong.[26]

Late that day, Jefferson and Madison left Floyd and the Unkechaug and traveled some 20 miles and lodged at Terry's, which Jefferson rated as "middling." On June 15, they visited Prince's nursery in Flushing. They lodged in Brooklyn and, on June 16, returned to New York via the ferry. Jefferson settled his expenses with Madison. He calculated the total at 153.51 dollars (over 5,000 dollars currently) and paid three-fifths of the costs. He owed Madison 25.94 dollars and on June 21 sent him a bank note. He likely spent the night with Madison and left for Philadelphia on June 17. He traveled as far as South Amboy, New Jersey. The next day he reached Allentown, Pennsylvania. He continued to make queries about the Hessian fly and completed his notes. On June 19, he stopped in Burlington, New Jersey, and visited a barber. He took Dunk's ferry across the Delaware River and arrived in Philadelphia. He had traveled 920 miles in thirty-three days.

AT POOSPATUCK: UNKECHAUG INDIANS (JUNE 14) 107

The next morning, Jefferson wrote Washington to inform the president that he was back: "Our tour was performed in somewhat less time than I had calculated. I have great hopes it has rid me of my head-ach, having scarcely had anything of it during my journey. Mister Madison's health is very visibly mended." Jefferson wrote James Monroe that Madison's "journey with me to the lakes placed him in better health than I have seen him." He also reported on his health to his daughter. He said he experienced "very perfect health" during the journey and that traveling had cleared his head of the "drudgery of business."[27]

He also told Madison that he had arrived back in Philadelphia. Madison was planning to travel to Massachusetts, and Jefferson encouraged him to collect leaf samples and make inquiries about the Hessian fly along the way. But Madison decided not to make the trip. He did not want to do it without a companion and other inconveniences, including his horse's illness and his dislike of stagecoach travel, weighed in the decision. Although Jefferson felt restored from the trip, Madison soon again suffered from fever and "symptoms of bile," which included nausea. That put an end to any thoughts of further travel. "I have given up . . . my trip," he informed Jefferson. As for the just completed journey with Jefferson, Madison told his father that it "was a very agreeable one, and carried us thro' an interesting Country new to us both."[28]

The business of secretary of state did not stop Jefferson from continuing to pursue the intellectual and scientific interests that the journey energized, whether the Hessian fly, the cultivation of sugar maple, or the compilation of Indian vocabularies.

As regards the latter, one of the first lists submitted on Jefferson's form came from the nearby reservation of the Delaware Indians named Brotherton, located in Burlington County. At the bottom of the form is written, "their numbers about forty years ago were about 280, are now about thirty." Jefferson's name appears on the sheet, but the form was not filled out by him. It is believed that Madison conducted the interviews in December 1792. If so, the first two vocabulary lists in what would become a growing collection were created by Jefferson and Madison.[29]

For the next two decades, Jefferson relied on a network of agents, travelers, missionaries, explorers, and friends to complete the forms and record the vocabularies of various tribes. He gave William Vans

108 A JOURNEY NORTH

Murray, a Maryland Congressman, the printed list in spring 1792, and Murray recorded the vocabulary of the Nanticoke. He asked William Linn, a director of the New York Missionary Society, to have missionaries use the form in their work with the Chickasaws. Jefferson introduced himself by letter to William Dunbar, a surveyor in Spanish West Florida, and asked him to procure responses from Creek, Chickasaw, Choctaw, and "tribes beyond the Mississippi." He asked David Campbell, a judge in Tennessee and commissioner of a boundary survey, if he could arrange for someone to record the vocabulary of the Cherokee.[30]

When he sent forms to John Sibley, a surgeon and Indian agent in New Orleans territory, he explained that he had been contemplating this project since "very early in life . . . and my course of life having given me opportunities of obtaining vocabularies of many Indian tribes, I have done so on my original plan, which tho' far from being perfect, has the valuable advantage of identity, & of thus bringing the languages to the same points of comparison." He undertook this labor while serving as president; politics would not displace philology.[31]

By 1800, when Jefferson wrote Campbell, the collection had grown. He told Dunbar, "I have at present about 30. tolerably full, among which the number radically different, is truly wonderful." Jefferson began to express fears of losing them. He informed Campbell, "I have now a large collection, & for fear that in case of any accident they should be lost, I am about to print them." The same day, March 14, he told Benjamin Hawkins, "I have now made up a large collection, and afraid to risk it any longer, lest by some accident it might be lost."[32]

Feeling that he now had a significant enough sample, Jefferson began to assemble his Comparative Vocabularies of Several Indian Languages. He wrote on both sides of approximately thirty pages. In one column on the left he listed the tribe: Shawnee, Nanticoke, Mohican, Unkechaug, Oneida, and so on. There were twenty-two in all. At the top of the page would be several English words from his list, and then he would fill in each column with the Indian word. "I have long been of opinion," he told Campbell, "that the only means we can have of coming at the descent and relations among the Indians, is by a collection & comparative view of their languages."[33]

Reviewing the material induced him to change his mind that all the orthography should be English. He realized trying to convert other languages into English would only compound the problem

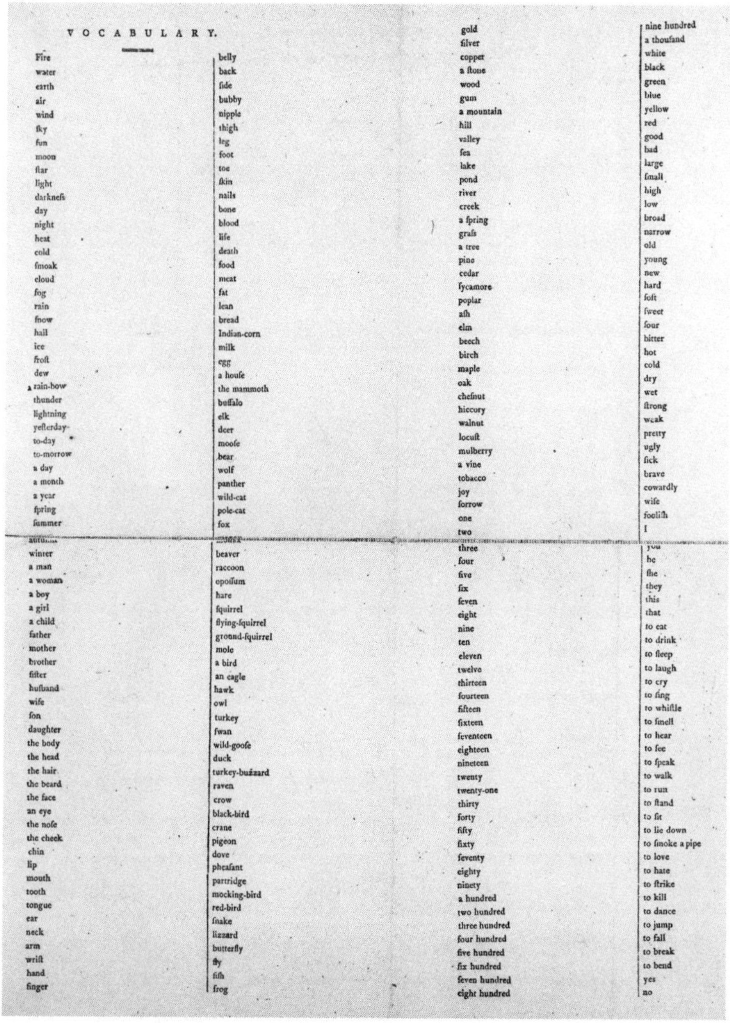

AT POOSPATUCK: UNKECHAUG INDIANS (JUNE 14) 109

Figure 9 Blank Vocabulary List (American Philosophical Society)

of transliteration. "I therefore think it best to keep them in the form of orthography in which they were taken," he told Dunbar, "only noting whether that were English, French, German or what." When John Pickering, linguist and lawyer, sent a copy of his *Essay on a Uniform Orthography for the Indian Languages of North America*, Jefferson expressed his hope that it would become the "uniform

Figure 10 Comparative Vocabularies of Several Indian Languages (American Philosophical Society)

AT POOSPATUCK: UNKECHAUG INDIANS (JUNE 14) III

orthography of the world," but doubted that local practices would be abandoned.[34]

He must have been overjoyed to receive vocabularies from Lewis and Clark and the Corps of Discovery Expedition in 1805. Jefferson had conceived the trip in 1803 when he secretly asked Congress for money (he feared Federalist opposition) to fund an expedition west to the Pacific for the purposes of commerce, exploration, and intercourse with Native peoples. The Louisiana Purchase had doubled the size of the United States that now extended to east of the Rocky Mountains. Jefferson chose Meriweather Lewis, a former U.S. Army captain and his personal secretary who spoke several Native languages, and William Clark, a retired officer who had served with Lewis, as leaders. Jefferson provided extensive instructions for what the Corps should accomplish and implored them to pay particular attention to acquiring knowledge of "the people inhabiting the line you will pursue," including "their language, traditions, monuments."[35]

In his list of requirements for the expedition, Lewis included "a number of printed vocabularies of the same words and form . . . with blank spaces for Indian words." Jefferson later recalled that Lewis "was very attentive to this instruction, never missing an opportunity of taking a vocabulary." In October 1804, before leaving St. Louis on the journey, Lewis had an army officer forward to Jefferson two vocabularies—first that of the Iowas and, five months later, the Sioux. Jefferson received another twelve in 1805, sent by barge from Fort Mandan. On his safe return to St. Louis in September 1806, Lewis informed Jefferson that he had collected an additional nine vocabularies, bringing the total to twenty-three.[36]

Jefferson was slow in completing his comparative vocabularies. In 1806, just as his collection grew, he discovered Pallas's work on Russian vocabulary and thought "by a comparison of language, to make the enquiry so long desired, as to the probability of a common origin between the people of colour of the two continents." Perhaps sensing that the president would be understandably delayed in completing the work, and wanting to profit from the massive public interest in adventures of the Corps of Discovery, Lewis asked permission to publish separately the ones he had gathered. Jefferson approved. Lewis's death by suicide in 1809 put an end to those plans.[37]

112   A JOURNEY NORTH

In May 1809, Jefferson's worst fears came to pass. His term as president having come to a close, Jefferson's twenty-nine trunks of possessions were loaded onto a boat docked overnight in Richmond, Virginia. One of the trunks, number 28, was stolen. The trunk, Jefferson noted, "may be described as a hair trunk of about 7. or 8. feet cubic contents, labelled on a card on the top TI. N° 28. containing principally writing paper of various qualities, but also some other articles of stationary, a pocket telescope with a brass case, a Dynamometer in steel and brass or instrument for measuring the exertions of draught animals, a collection of vocabularies of the Indian languages, & some other articles not particularly noted in the memorandum taken." Jefferson's cousin George placed an ad in the *Richmond Enquirer* offering a 20-dollar reward. By June, he had learned that someone had purchased the trunk for 3 dollars from a "negro waterman [who] says he found it broken open." The waterman was a slave named Ned, who was tried, found guilty, and the court ordered "that he be burnt in the left hand and receive thirty-nine lashes on his bare back at the public whipping post." It is unclear whether the man who purchased the trunk was also tried, though Jefferson's cousin wrote that he requested to have him prosecuted "for dealing with a negro for things which he must have known were stolen."[38]

Jefferson explained what had happened in a letter to Benjamin Smith Barton, an eminent physician and naturalist, who in 1797 had published *New Views of the Origin of the Tribes and Nations of America* and was inquiring about obtaining copies of some of Lewis's vocabularies for a new edition. His melancholy is evident:

> [A]n irreparable misfortune has deprived me of them. I have now been thirty years availing myself of every possible opportunity of procuring Indian vocabularies to the same set of words: my opportunities were probably better than will ever occur again to any person having the same desire. I had collected about 50. and had digested most of them in collateral columns and meant to have printed them the last year of my stay in Washington. but not having yet digested Cap' Lewis's collection, nor having leisure then to do it, I put it off till I should return home. the whole, as well digest as originals were packed in a trunk of stationary & sent round by water with about 30. other packages of my effects from

AT POOSPATUCK: UNKECHAUG INDIANS (JUNE 14)   113

Washington, and while ascending James river, this package, on account of it's weight & presumed precious contents, was singled out & stolen. the thief being disappointed on opening it, threw into the river all it's contents of which he thought he could make no use. among these were the whole of the vocabularies. some leaves floated ashore & were found in the mud; but these were very few, & so defaced by the mud & water that no general use can ever be made of them.[39]

Jefferson lost most of the original Indian vocabularies in his possession, as well as his copies of the Lewis and Clark vocabularies, except for a "morsel" of "Capt Lewis's of the Pani language." Jefferson repeated the last phrase: "no general use can ever be made of the wrecks of my loss" and concluded he was too old to make much progress on another attempt to gather vocabularies. In October 1809, after his death, Lewis's surviving papers, including the vocabularies, passed to Clark, who brought them to Philadelphia for publication.

From there, the story of the Lewis and Clark vocabularies becomes murky. Clark left them with Nicholas Biddle, who would edit the journals of the expedition and publish them in 1814. Biddle lent the vocabularies to Barton, who reassured Jefferson "that they shall be taken good care of." Barton died in 1815, and at that point the Indian vocabularies disappeared. Biddle claimed they were not returned to him, and the mystery has never been resolved. In 1817, Jefferson donated his surviving collection to the American Philosophical Society. He sent the ones that had escaped the thieves in 1809, or been collected since, as well as the fragments "which were gathered up on the banks of the river where they had been strewed by the plunderers of the trunk in which they were." Included in his donation was the Unkechaug list as well as the mud-stained pages of the comparative vocabularies. He told Peter Du Ponceau, the Society's vice president, "If you can recover Capt Lewis's collection, they will make an important addition, for there was no part of his instructions which he executed more fully or carefully, never meeting with a single Indian of a new tribe, without making his vocabulary the 1st object." They remain lost.[40]

Jefferson maintained his lifelong interest in Indian languages. He forwarded a copy of the vocabulary of the Nottoway tribe to Du Ponceau, who replied that "among the Vocabularies which you

114 A JOURNEY NORTH

before had the Goodness to send to the Historical Committee, there is none of this language, nor of any connected with it." That lack of connection had already begun to discomfit Jefferson. Perhaps his interest in demonstrating links between languages in searching for origins was mistaken. More than half the languages he had collected "differed as radically, each from every other, as the Greek, the Latin & Islandic. and even of those which seemed to be derived from the same Radix, the departure was such that the tribes speaking them could not probably understand one another." In 1825, he wrote, "I am persuaded that among the tribes on our two continents a great number of languages, radically different, will be found. it will be curious to consider how so many, so radically different, have been preserved, by such small tribes, in coterminous settlements of moderate extent." He recalled having collected vocabularies that were unfortunately lost, but in his initial attempts to "arrange them into families and dialects, I found, in one instance, that about half a dozen might be so classed; in another three or four; but I am sure that a third at least, if not more, were perfectly insulated from each other." He concluded, "I believe we shall find it impossible to translate our language into any of the Indian, or any of theirs into ours."[41]

In 1824, a professor at Transylvania University, in Lexington, Kentucky, wrote Jefferson, requesting assistance gathering Indian vocabularies. Jefferson was tired, and probably no longer wanted to be reminded of a largely lost and failed project. "I am become from age and debility so entirely unequal to the labor of writing," he replied, "that I have been obliged to withdraw from all correspondence whatever, it is time for me to resign to younger hands the cares of literature."[42]

If Jefferson's study of Indian vocabularies failed to produce the results he expected, it provided an unexpected benefit. Never would he have imagined that the vocabularies he collected in the eighteenth century might allow Native tribes in the twenty-first century to reclaim their lost languages. In 2010, Chief Harry Wallace of the Unkechaug Nation announced an effort to revive the language. To do so, Unkechaug scholars would examine land deeds and legal documents, religious records, and word lists. Paramount to their efforts were the 201 words Jefferson recorded in June 1791, listing them on the back of a piece of paper he had pulled from his pocket.[43]

Epilogue: Farewells

On June 2, 1792, Jefferson purchased a portrait of Madison by Robert Edge Pine, an English painter living in Philadelphia. Pine had died in 1788, and Jefferson bought the painting from Pine's widow for 33 dollars. He added it to his collection of "principal American characters," which included Washington and Adams—though not Hamilton. Unfortunately, the painting is lost, and most of Pine's other work was destroyed by a fire in 1803.

In 1806, Madison acquired a copy of a portrait of Jefferson executed the previous year by Gilbert Stuart. Stuart was America's foremost portraitist, producing over a thousand paintings, including his iconic unfinished depiction of George Washington. Stuart also painted Madison. Appointed by Jefferson in 1804 to serve as minister plenipotentiary to the court of Spain, James Bowdoin commissioned the companion portraits of the president and his secretary of state, portraits that, a scholar notes, "show how Jefferson and Madison became more in partnership than either would have been alone." Asked to lend it in 1831, Madison refused, saying he was "unwilling to expose the Portrait of Mr. Jefferson by Stuart, to the casualties however slight, to a removal to a distance however small."[1]

Their partnership and friendship only deepened in the thirty-five years they had together after their northern journey. Jefferson resigned as secretary of state in 1793, having had enough of "the hated occupation of politics." He offered Madison assorted reasons: his health had broken down; his ambition had evaporated; he had enough of the poison of political opposition; he desired tranquility; he "set less store by a posthumous than present name." Since

Figure 11 Gilbert Stuart, "Portrait of Thomas Jefferson," ca. 1805–1807 (Bowdoin College Museum of Art)

we know he would soon enough return to serve, as vice president and president no less, it is easy to view him as protesting too much. Yet he relished his brief life in retirement and told Madison, "I shall never take another newspaper of any sort. I find my mind totally absorbed in my rural occupations."[2]

Madison, too, considered retirement. Domestic life had its appeals (Dolley called him "the great little Madison"). Jefferson implored

Figure 12 Gilbert Stuart, "Portrait of James Madison," ca. 1805–1807 (Bowdoin College Museum of Art)

Madison to reconsider as, in the minds of many, there was "no greater affliction than the fear of your retirement." Indeed, rather than retire, Madison should compete for "a more splendid and a more efficacious post"—the presidency. Reasons of *"every kind,"* Madison responded, prevented him from considering it. Soon enough, Madison would help engineer Jefferson's return to politics in the election of 1796. Hearing that Madison planned to retire, a

118   EPILOGUE

bemused John Adams observed, "It Seems the Mode of becoming great is to retire. Madison I Suppose after a Retirement of a few years is to become President or V.P. . . . It is marvelous how political Plants grow in the shade."[3]

While Jefferson served as vice president, it was Madison's turn to play the role of retired statesman. Then, after each completed two terms as president (with Madison serving as Jefferson's secretary of state), Jefferson retired to Monticello in 1809 and Madison to Montpelier in 1817.

Jefferson kept busy in retirement with countless tasks, none of which mattered to him as much as the establishment of the University of Virginia. Jefferson had always understood education to be the key to protecting liberty, which meant that "the people are the only safe depositories of their own liberty, & that they are not safe unless enlightened to a certain degree." Only education could safeguard liberty.[4]

In the 1770s, he had proposed in Virginia "A Bill for the More General Diffusion of Knowledge" and over the decades contemplated the creation of a university in Virginia. Only in 1814 did the plan begin to gain traction. Madison joined the project, and months after leaving office, he attended a meeting of the Board of Visitors of Central College, which would morph into the University of Virginia. Having not written much to one another in the last years of Madison's presidency due to the toll on Madison caused by the War of 1812 (Jefferson described it as a period of "incessant labors, corroding anxieties, active enemies and interested friends"), their correspondence increased and was filled with discussions of the university. Jefferson sent Madison drafts of his report on Central College and adopted Madison's suggested revisions (for example, not to mention recruiting professors from abroad as it might excite prejudice). Both men signed the final report, as did James Monroe.[5]

Once the legislature approved the creation of the university, Jefferson and Madison served on the Board of Visitors, and Jefferson was elected first rector. The University of Virginia was Jefferson's creation, from the curriculum to the faculty to the architecture of the "academical village" that he envisioned. Madison was his partner and supporter. Jefferson took comfort that, when he passed, he could leave the institution under his friend's care. Indeed, on Jefferson's death, Madison was elected rector.[6]

EPILOGUE 119

In their final years, each dealt with setbacks to his health. Madison complained of fevers, colds, and seizures; Jefferson endured a likely staph infection that nearly killed him, and he suffered a fall in which he broke his left arm. They visited each other when they could, and in their correspondence, they often looked backward toward the Declaration of Independence, the meaning of the Constitution, and Washington's legacy, among other topics, in the history of the Revolution and early republic. And they continued to discuss university matters.

Each had occasion to recall the journey they took together in 1791, more than thirty years earlier. When Margaret Bayard Smith, Washington doyenne and writer, visited Madison in 1828, she noted that he offered "a stream of history . . . rich in sentiments and facts, so enlivened by anecdotes and epigrammatic remarks . . . it was living History!"[7]

Two years later, Smith asked Madison for anecdotes about his relationship with Jefferson and the journey they had taken together. She mentioned that Jefferson had shown her his "little journal—kept in a little book of birch-bark."[8]

Madison replied that the two had been strangers until 1776 and that "among the occasions which made us immediate companions was the trip in 1791, to the borders of Canada." He continued, "according to an understanding between us, the observations in our way through the Northern part of N. York, and the newly settled entirety of Vermont, to be noted by him were of a miscellaneous cast, and were in part at least noted on the Birch bark of which you speak. The few observations devolving on me, related chiefly to agricultural & Economic objects. On recurring to them, I find the only interest they contain is in the comparison they may afford of the infant state with the present growth of the settlements through which we passed."

Madison explained that "the scenes & subjects which had occurred during the Session of Congress which had just terminated at our departure from New York, entered of course into our itinerary conversations," and he offered an anecdote:

The new Constitution of the U. States having been just put into operation, Forms of Government were the uppermost topics every where, more especially at a Convivial board. And the question being started as to the best mode of providing the Executive

Chief, it was, among other opinions, boldly advanced that a hereditary designation was preferable to any elective process that could be devised. At the close of an eloquent effussion against the agitations and animosities of a popular choice, and in behalf of birth, as on the whole, affording even a better chance for a suitable head of the Government, Mr. Jefferson, with a smile remarked that he had heard of a University somewhere in which the Professorship of Mathematics was hereditary. The reply, received with acclamation, was a coup de grace to the Anti Republican Heretic.[9]

It is a delightful story. Politics must have surfaced in dinner conversations, even if it was an escape from the politics of the moment that had powered the journey. We can only guess at whose "Convivial board" this exchange took place; perhaps it was while dining with Philip Schuyler and others in Albany.

Jefferson also had occasion to recall the trip. In 1825, he wrote about it to his granddaughter, Ellen Wayles Randolph Coolidge. A favorite of Jefferson's, Ellen met and married a Boston businessman at Monticello on May 27, 1825, and, on their way to Boston, the couple toured New York and New England. On August 1, she wrote her "dearest grandfather" to tell him about the journey. Their trip took them "up the Hudson as far as Albany from thence to Saratoga, Lakes George and Champlain; as far north as Burlington in Vermont, from Burlington across the country to the Connecticut River; & down this river to Springfield; from whence, through the interior of Massachusetts to Boston."

Ellen went on to say pointedly that the journey "has given me an idea of prosperity & improvement, such as I fear our Southern States cannot hope for, whilst the canker of slavery eats into their hearts, & diseases the whole body by this ulcer at the core. when I consider the immense advantages of soil & climate which we possess over these people, it grieves me to think that such great gifts of Nature should have failed to produce any thing like the wealth and improvement which the New-Englanders have wrung from the hard bosom of a stubborn & ungrateful land, & amid the gloom & desolation of their wintry skies." It was a striking indictment of the South and a paean to the superiority of the free-labor North.[10]

In his response, Jefferson acknowledged his granddaughter's condemnation of Southern society: "I have no doubt you will find also

EPILOGUE   121

the state of society there more congenial with your mind, than the rustic scenes you have left: altho these do not want their points of endearment. nay, one single circumstance changed, and their scale would hardly be the lightest. one fatal stain deforms what nature had bestowed on us of her fairest gifts." The "one single circumstance" that changed was the gradual abolition of slavery in Massachusetts.[11]

Fatal stain. Two years earlier he called slavery a "hideous blot." He always knew slavery was wrong. "I tremble for my country when I reflect that God is just; that his justice cannot sleep forever," he wrote in 1781–1782. Believing in racial inferiority and that Blacks and whites could not live together peaceably, he supported gradual emancipation and colonization. The Missouri crisis of 1820, which made clear the geographical division of slave and free states, alarmed him anew. "We have the wolf by the ear," he wrote, "and we can neither hold him nor safely let him go. Justice is on one scale, and self-preservation in the other." He confessed in his autobiography, "nothing is more certainly written in the book of fate than that these people are to be free." He added, "nor is it less certain that the two races, equally free, cannot live in the same government."[12]

In his letter to his granddaughter, after briefly alluding to slavery, he turned his attention to more congenial thoughts. He recalled his trip with Madison and used it to reflect on the glory of free government and mankind's happiness:

> I am glad you took the delightful tour which you describe in your letter. it is almost exactly that which mr Madison and myself pursued in May and June 1791. setting out from Philadelphia, our course was to N: York, up the Hudson to Albany, Troy, Saratoga, F^t Edward, F^t George, L. George Ticonderoga, Crown point, penetrated into L. Champlain, returned the same way to Saratoga, thence crossed the mountains to Bennington, Northampton, along Connecticut river to it's mouth, crossed the Sound into Long-island, and along it's Northern margin to Brooklyn, re-crossed to N. York and returned. but, from Saratoga till we got back to Northampton, was then mostly desert. now it is what 34. years of free and good government have made it. it shews how soon the labor of man would make a paradise of the whole earth, were it not for misgovernment, & a diversion of all

122 EPILOGUE

his energies from their proper object, the happiness of man, to the selfish interests of kings, nobles and priests.[13]

Time was running short for the octogenarian. "Now far gone in my 83d year," he wrote on New Year's Day 1826. On April 3 and 4, he and Madison met for the final time at a Board of Visitors session in Charlottesville. In discussing university matters, Jefferson had told Madison that when he was removed "beyond the bourne of life itself, as I soon must, it is a comfort to leave that institution under your care."[14]

By the time they met for a final time, they had already exchanged valedictory letters expressing their deep and profound affection for one another. Jefferson wrote, "the friendship which has subsisted between us, now half a century, and the harmony of our political principles and pursuits, have been sources of constant happiness to me thro' that long period." It also gave him "great solace" that Madison was "engaged in vindicating to posterity the course we have pursued for preserving to them, *in all their purity*, the blessings of self-government, which we had assisted too in acquiring for them." Jefferson was contemplating how the future would judge all that he had done in the nation's service. The letter closed, "take care of me when dead, and be assured that I shall leave with you my last affections."[15]

Madison replied a week later:

> You cannot look back to the long period of our private friendship & political harmony, with more affecting recollections than I do. If they are a source of pleasure to you, what ought they not be to me? We can not be deprived of the happy consciousness of the pure devotion to the public good, with which we discharged the trusts committed to us. And I indulge a confidence that sufficient evidence will find its way to another generation, to ensure, after we are gone, whatever of justice may be witheld whilst we are here. . . . Wishing & hoping that you may yet live to increase the debt which our Country owes you, and to witness the increasing gratitude, which alone can pay it, I offer you the fullest return of affectionate assurances.[16]

Jefferson died on July 4, 1826. Madison lived for another decade. During that time, he honored his friend's final wish and became a caretaker of his memory, corresponding with biographers, setting the record straight, resurrecting Jefferson to comment on the momentous political questions of the day—tariffs and nullification. Of course, in doing so, Madison was also safeguarding his own legacy. No erroneous accounts of Jefferson's beliefs or life, however significant or trifling, went unchallenged. When the governor of Virginia suggested that Jefferson opposed protective tariffs, Madison made clear that Jefferson had never denied their constitutionality. When a writer sent Madison a copy of his biography of Jefferson, Madison offered a correction: Jefferson's hair was "not *red*, but between *yellow & red*."[17]

In his will, Jefferson left Madison his walking stick: "I give to my friend James Madison of Montpelier my gold-mounted walking staff of animal horn, as a token of the cordial and affectionate friendship which for nearly now an half century, has united us in the same principles and pursuits of what we have deemed for the greatest good of our country."[18]

On receiving it, Madison wrote Thomas Jefferson Randolph, Jefferson's grandson, that he accepted it "with all the feelings due to

Figure 13 Jefferson's Walking Stick (Thomas Jefferson Foundation at Monticello)

124 EPILOGUE

such a token of the place I held in the friendship of one, whom I so much revered & loved when living and whose memory can never cease to be dear to me." On his death, Madison bequeathed it back to Randolph. It is now on permanent loan to the Thomas Jefferson Foundation.[19]

The walking stick, gold mounted and made of bone, paid tribute to the many miles they had traveled in one another's company. As long as they were together, they were never out of their way.

Acknowledgments

Founders Online is a remarkable archive of the writings of seven leading Revolutionary figures, including Jefferson and Madison. It was created by the National Historical Publications & Records Commission, and it is a treasure that allowed me to work as long as I had an Internet connection. I am also indebted to J. Jefferson Looney of the Papers of Thomas Jefferson and J. C. A. Stagg of the Papers of James Madison for their assistance with various inquiries.

In Spring 2021, Ava Feldman took my cultural history course and soon thereafter became my research assistant. Without her, I could not have completed this book. Alexandra Paskhaver, another talented undergraduate, also conducted research. Both have bright futures ahead, one as a lawyer, the other as a writer.

I am lucky for a group of friends and colleagues who commented on all or part of the manuscript: Bob Allison, Carla Cevasco, Jonathan Freedman, Jim Goodman, Doug Greenberg, Peter Mancall, Peter Onuf, Aaron Sachs, and Tom Slaughter. I go back over forty years with a few of these folks, who have read drafts of all my books. They have done much more than that, and it is impossible to find words other than simply thank you for always being there.

This is my third book with Tim Bent at Oxford University Press. I am grateful for his enthusiasm and skillful editing and thrilled that he let me get away this time with long quotes from the sources. My thanks to Egle Zigaite for shepherding the book through production and to Rachel Perkins for her beautiful jacket design. The talented illustrator Katherine Messenger drew the map of the journey. My agent Zoe Pagnamenta, at Calligraphlit, made the

ACKNOWLEDGMENTS

introduction—just one of the many ways she has represented me so well for so many years.

When we are not talking about the Yankees or golf, Dave Masur, Mark Richman, and Bruce Rossky occasionally ask me what I am writing before quickly changing the subject. I love them for that and so much more.

While working on this book, I became a grandfather. Sophie and Garrett Jaffe had Evan in May 2020 and Henry in December 2021. Ben and Rachel Masur delivered Ethan and Jason in July 2021. Four spectacular boys, impossible to imagine when Jani and I went on our first date fifty years ago. It was 1975, and that fall "Born to Run" filled the airwaves. Our whole life, love has been wild, love has been real. And now, with our children and grandchildren, we have gotten to that place where we really want to go. It's time to walk in the sun.

This book is for my grandsons and their lifelong journey. With all my love, Grandpa.

Notes

PREFACE

1. James Madison to Margaret Bayard Smith, September 21, 1830, https://founders.archives.gov/documents/Madison/99-02-02-2160
2. The letters are collected in James Morton Smith, ed., *The Republic of Letters: The Correspondence between Thomas Jefferson and James Madison, 1776–1826*, 3 vols. (New York: W.W. Norton, 1995).
3. John Quincy Adams, *The Jubilee of the Constitution* (New York: Samuel Colman, 1839), p. 111.

PROLOGUE: TRAVELERS

1. Thomas Jefferson to John Page, January 20, 1763, https://founders.archives.gov/documents/Jefferson/01-01-02-0003. On Jefferson as a traveler, see Edward Dumbauld, *Thomas Jefferson: American Tourist* (Norman: University of Oklahoma Press, 1946).
2. Jefferson, Notes of a Tour of English Gardens, [April 2–14] 1786, https://founders.archives.gov/documents/Jefferson/01-09-02-0328
3. Jefferson, Notes of a Tour into the Southern Parts of France, &C., March 3–June 10, 1787, https://founders.archives.gov/documents/Jefferson/01-11-02-0389; Jefferson to John Bannister, June 19, 1787, https://founders.archives.gov/documents/Jefferson/01-11-02-0406; Jefferson to William Short, March 27, 1787, https://founders.archives.gov/documents/Jefferson/01-11-02-0242. See George Green Shackleford, *Thomas Jefferson's Travels in Europe, 1784–1789* (Baltimore: Johns Hopkins University Press, 1998), and Annette Gordon-Reed and Peter S. Onuf, *"Most Blessed of the Patriarchs": Thomas Jefferson and the Empire of the Imagination* (New York: Liveright, 2016), pp. 97–166.

128 NOTES

4. Jefferson, Notes on a Tour through Holland and the Rhine Valley, March 3–April 23, 1788, https://founders.archives.gov/documents/Jefferson/01-13-02-0003

5. Jefferson's Hints to Americans Traveling in Europe, June 19, 1788, https://founders.archives.gov/documents/Jefferson/01-13-02-0173

6. Jefferson to Peter Carr, August 10, 1787, https://founders.archives.gov/documents/Jefferson/01-12-02-0021

7. Jefferson to Madison, December 8, 1784, https://founders.archives.gov/documents/Jefferson/01-07-02-0402

8. Madison to Jefferson, April 27, 1785, https://founders.archives.gov/documents/Madison/01-08-02-0146

9. James Monroe to Madison, July 12, 1785, https://founders.archives.gov/documents/Madison/01-08-02-0170; Madison to Monroe, July 28, 1785, https://founders.archives.gov/?q=%20Author%3A%-22Madison%2C%20James%22%20Recipient%3A%22Monroe%2C%20James%22&s=1111311111&r=14

10. Madison to Jefferson, September 7, 1784, https://founders.archives.gov/?q=%20Author%3A%22Madison%2C%20James%22%20Recipient%3A%22Jefferson%2C%20Thomas%22&s=1111311111&r=85

11. Madison to James Madison, Sr., September 6, 1784, https://founders.archives.gov/documents/Madison/01-08-02-0060; Madison to Jefferson, September 7, 1784, https://founders.archives.gov-/?q=%20Author%3A%22Madison%2C%20James%22%20Recipient%3A%22Jefferson%2C%20Thomas%22&s=1111311111&r=85. See J. Bennett Nolan, *Lafayette in America Day by Day* (Baltimore: Johns Hopkins University Press, 1934). On Madison's earlier trip, see Ralph Ketcham, *James Madison: A Biography* (New York: Macmillan, 1971), p. 60.

12. Madison to Jefferson, October 11, 1784, https://founders.archives.gov/documents/Madison/01-08-02-0063; Madison to Jefferson, October 17, 1784, https://founders.archives.gov/documents/Madison/01-08-02-0064

13. Madison to James Monroe, November 14, 1784, https://founders.archives.gov/?q=%20Author%3A%22Madison%2C%20James%22%20Recipient%3A%22Monroe%2C%20James%22&s=1111311111&r=1; Madison to Jefferson, October 17, 1784, https://founders.archives.gov/documents/Madison/01-08-02-0064; Jefferson to Madison, December 8, 1784, https://founders.archives.gov/documents/Jefferson/01-07-02-0402; Madison to Jefferson, October 3, 1785, https://founders.archives.gov/documents/Jefferson/01-07-02-0402

NOTES 129

BEFORE THE JOURNEY

1. Abigail Adams to Cotton Tufts, September 8, 1784, https://found ers.archives.gov/documents/Adams/04-05-02-0236; Alexander White to Mary Wood, March 8, 1789, https://rotunda.upress.virgi nia.edu/founders/default.xqy?keys=FFCP-chron-1780-1789-03-08 -5&mode=deref

2. Madison to Ambrose Madison, March 1, 1791, https://founders. archives.gov/?q=1791%20Author%3A%22Madison%2C%20Ja mes%22&s=1111311111&r=71; Madison to James Monroe, April 12, 1791, https://founders.archives.gov/documents/Madi son/01-14-02-0006; Madison, "Notes on Hudson Valley Lodgings," after April 24, 1791, https://founders.archives.gov/documents/Madi son/01-14-02-0013; Jefferson to Madison, May 9, 1791, https://found ers.archives.gov/documents/Madison/01-14-02-0015; Madison to Jefferson, May 12, 1791, https://founders.archives.gov/documents/ Madison/01-14-02-0018

3. Jefferson to George Washington, May 15, 1791, https://founders. archives.gov/documents/Washington/05-08-02-0146; Jefferson to Martha Jefferson Randolph, June 23, 1791, https://found ers.archives.gov/?q=%22headach%22%20Author%3A%22Je fferson%2C%20Thomas%22&s=1111311111&r=11&sr=; Jefferson to William Fleming, March 20, 1764, https://found ers.archives.gov/?q=%E2%80%9Ca%20violent%20head%20 ach%E2%80%9D&s=1111311111&sa=&r=1&sr=; Jefferson to William Short, March 1, 1784, https://founders.archives.gov- /?q=%22attack%20of%20my%20periodical%22&s=1111311 111&sa=&r=1&sr=; Jefferson to Martha Jefferson Randolph, June 6, 1790, https://founders.archives.gov/?q=%E2%80%9Cviol ent%E2%80%9D%20%20Author%3A%22Jefferson%2C%20Tho mas%22%20Dates-From%3A1790-05-01&s=1111311111&r=1; Jefferson to Albert Gallatin, March 20, 1807, https://founders.archi ves.gov/?q=%E2%80%9Cobliged%20to%20be%20shut%20up%20 in%20a%20dark%20room%20from%20early%20in%20the%20f orenoon%20till%20night%2C%20with%20a%20periodical%20h ead-ache.%E2%80%9D&s=1111311111&sa=&r=1&sr=

4. Right Reverend James Madison to Madison, April 10, 1791, https:// founders.archives.gov/?q=impairing%20Recipient%3A%22Madi son%2C%20James%22&s=1111311111&r=3; Madison, *Autobiography*, December 1830, https://founders.archives.gov/?q=feebleness%20Aut hor%3A%22Madison%2C%20James%22&s=1111311111&r=8&sr=

130 NOTES

5. Madison to William Bradford, November 9, 1772, https://founders. archives.gov/documents/Madison/01-01-02-0015

6. Jefferson to Madison, March 16, 1784, https://founders.archives. gov/documents/Jefferson/01-07-02-0032; Madison to Jefferson, January 10, 1801, https://founders.archives.gov/documents/Madi son/01-17-02-0300; Madison to Samuel H. Smith, November 4, 1826, https://founders.archives.gov/documents/Madison/04-04-02-0163; Jefferson to Thomas C. Flourney, October 1, 1812, https://found ers.archives.gov/documents/Jefferson/03-05-02-0312

7. Jefferson to John Adams, June 10, 1815, https://founders.archives. gov/documents/Jefferson/03-08-02-0425; Jefferson to Madison, May 8, 1784, https://founders.archives.gov/documents/Jeffer son/01-07-02-0179; and see list from Jefferson to Madison, September 1, 1785, https://founders.archives.gov/documents/Jeffer son/01-08-02-0360; Madison to Samuel H. Smith, November 4, 1826, https://founders.archives.gov/documents/Madison/04-04-02-0163;

8. Jefferson to James Monroe, May 20, 1782, https://founders.archives. gov/documents/Jefferson/01-06-02-0174

9. Madison to Edmund Randolph, June 11, 1782, https://founders.archi ves.gov/?q=%20Author%3A%22Madison%2C%20James%22%20Re cipient%3A%22Randolph%2C%20Edmund%22&s=1111311 111&r=15

10. Jefferson to Marquis de Chastellux, November 26, 1782, https:// founders.archives.gov/documents/Jefferson/01-06-02-0192, Also see Edmund Randolph to Madison, September 20, 1782, in which he describes Jefferson's grief as "violent," https://founders.archives. gov/documents/Madison/01-05-02-0063

11. Jefferson to Madison, August 31, 1783, https://founders.archives. gov/documents/Jefferson/01-06-02-0262

12. Madison to Edmund Randolph, December 2, 1782, https://found ers.archives.gov/documents/Madison/01-05-02-0149; Madison to Jefferson, February 11, 1783, https://founders.archives.gov/docume nts/Jefferson/01-06-02-0218; Jefferson to Madison, January 30, 1787, https://founders.archives.gov/?q=%20Author%3A%22Jeffer son%2C%20Thomas%22%20Recipient%3A%22Madison%2C%20Ja mes%22&s=1111311111&r=72

13. Jefferson to Madison, May 11, 1785, https://founders.archives.gov- /?q=%20Author%3A%22Jefferson%2C%20Thomas%22%20Recipi ent%3A%22Madison%2C%20James%22&s=1111311111&r=54

NOTES

131

14. Jefferson to Peter Carr, December 11, 1783, https://founders.archi ves.gov/documents/Jefferson/01-06-02-0302

15. Jefferson to Madison, August 31, 1783, https://founders.archives. gov/?q=%20Author%3A%22Jefferson%2C%20Thomas%22%20Re cipient%3A%22Madison%2C%20James%22&s=1111311111&r=26

16. Jefferson to Madison, February 20, 1784, https://founders.archives. gov/?q=%20Author%3A%22Jefferson%2C%20Thomas%22%20Re cipient%3A%22Madison%2C%20James%22&s=1111311111&r=32

17. Jefferson to Chastellux, November 26, 1782, https://founders. archives.gov/documents/Jefferson/01-06-02-0192; Ellen Coolidge quoted in Annette Gordon Reed and Peter Onuf, *"Most Blessed of the Patriarchs": Thomas Jefferson and the Empire of the Imagination* (New York: Liveright, 2016), pp. 98–99; Thomas Jefferson to James Madison, August 13, 1801, https://founders.archives.gov-/?q=chess%20Author%3A%22Jefferson%2C%20Thomas%22&s=111 1311111&r=12&sr=

18. Madison to Jefferson, March 16, 1784, https://founders.archives. gov/documents/Madison/01-08-02-0002; Jefferson to Monroe, May 11, 1785, https://founders.archives.gov/documents/Jeffer son/01-08-02-0096

19. Madison to Jefferson, March 16, 1784, https://founders.archives.gov/ documents/Madison/01-08-02-0002; Jefferson to Madison, June 17, 1783, https://founders.archives.gov/?q=%20Author%3A%22Jeffer son%2C%20Thomas%22%20Recipient%3A%22Madison%2C%20Ja mes%22&s=1111311111&r=24

20. Madison to Jefferson, December 4, 1786, https://founders.archives. gov/?q=%20Author%3A%22Madison%2C%20James%22%20Recipi ent%3A%22Jefferson%2C%20Thomas%22&s=1111311111&r=117; Jefferson to Madison, December 16, 1786, https://founders.archi ves.gov/?q=Recipient%3A%22Madison%2C%20James%22%20Aut hor%3A%22Jefferson%2C%20Thomas%22&s=1111311111&r=70

21. Madison to Jefferson, April 23, 1787, https://founders.archives.gov/ documents/Madison/01-09-02-0217. On Shays's Rebellion, see Leonard Richards, *Shays's Rebellion: The American Revolution's Final Battle* (Philadelphia: University of Pennsylvania Press, 2003).

22. Jefferson to Madison, January 30, 1787, https://founders.archives. gov/documents/Madison/01-09-02-0126

23. Madison to Jefferson, July 18, 1787, https://founders.archives.gov/ documents/Madison/01-10-02-0062

132 NOTES

24. Jefferson to John Adams, November 13, 1787, https://founders.archi
ves.gov/documents/Jefferson/01-12-02-0342; Jefferson to William
Stephens Smith, November 13, 1787, https://founders.archives.gov/
documents/Jefferson/01-12-02-0348

25. "The Federalist Papers: No. 84," https://avalon.law.yale.edu/18th_
century/fed84.asp

26. Jefferson to Madison, December 20, 1787, https://founders.archives.
gov/?q=%20Author%3A%22Jefferson%2C%20Thomas%22%20Re
cipient%3A%22Madison%2C%20James%22&s=1111311111&r=86;
Madison to Jefferson, October 17, 1788, https://founders.archives.
gov/?q=%20Author%3A%22Madison%2C%20James%22%20Recipi
ent%3A%22Jefferson%2C%20Thomas%22&s=1111311111&r=160;
Madison to Jefferson, March 15, 1789, https://founders.archives.gov-
/?q=%20Author%3A%22Jefferson%2C%20Thomas%22%20Recipi
ent%3A%22Madison%2C%20James%22&s=1111311111&r=105

27. Jefferson to Madison, January 9, 1790, https://founders.archives.
gov/?q=%20Author%3A%22Jefferson%2C%20Thomas%22%20Re
cipient%3A%22Madison%2C%20James%22&s=1111311111&r=122;
George W. Corner, ed., *The Autobiography of Benjamin Rush*
(Westport, CT: Greenwood Press, 1970), p. 181.

28. Jefferson to James Monroe, June 20, 1790, https://founders.archi
ves.gov/documents/Jefferson/01-16-02-0312; Jefferson to Thomas
Mann Randolph, Jr., June 20, 1790, https://founders.archives.gov/
documents/Jefferson/01-16-02-0314

29. Madison to Henry Lee, April 13, 1790, https://founders.archives.
gov/?q=%20Author%3A%22Madison%2C%20James%22%20Re
cipient%3A%22Lee%2C%20Henry%22%20Dates-From%3A1
790-04-11&s=1111311111&r=1; Jefferson to John Taylor, May
28, 1816, https://founders.archives.gov/documents/Jeffer
son/03-10-02-0053; Discrimination between Present and Original
Holders of the Public Debt, [February 11] 1790, https://founders.
archives.gov/documents/Madison/01-13-02-0030

30. Report Relative to a Provision for the Support of Public Credit,
[January 9, 1790], https://founders.archives.gov/documents/Hamil
ton/01-06-02-0076-0002-0001; Chernow, p. 288.

31. Assumption of the State Debts, [April 22] 1790, https://founders.
archives.gov/documents/Madison/01-13-02-0117

32. Madison to James Monroe, April 17, 1790, https://founders.archi
ves.gov/documents/Madison/01-13-02-0109; Assumption of the

NOTES 133

State Debts, [April 22] 1790, https://founders.archives.gov/docume
nts/Madison/01-13-02-0117

33. Jefferson to Monroe, June 20, 1790, https://founders.archives.gov/
documents/Jefferson/01-16-02-0312; Jefferson to Thomas Mann
Randolph, Jr., June 20, 1790, https://founders.archives.gov/docume
nts/Jefferson/01-16-02-0314

34. Jefferson's Account of the Bargain on the Assumption and Residence
Bills, [1792?], https://founders.archives.gov/documents/Jeffer
son/01-17-02-0018-0012

35. Jefferson's Account of the Bargain on the Assumption and Residence
Bills, [1792?], https://founders.archives.gov/documents/Jeffer
son/01-17-02-0018-0012; Thomas Jefferson, "The Anas," in *The
Writings of Thomas Jefferson. V.1.*, p. 275, https://babel.hathitrust.org/
cgi/pt?id=hvd.32044010456762&view=1up&seq=341&skin=2021;
Jefferson to David Ramsay, June 27, 1790, https://founders.archives.
gov/documents/Jefferson/01-16-02-0339

36. Jefferson's Account of the Bargain on the Assumption and Residence
Bills, [1792?], https://founders.archives.gov/documents/Jeffer
son/01-17-02-0018-0012; James Madison to George Washington,
August 24, 1788, https://founders.archives.gov/documents/Was
hington/04-06-02-0423; Jefferson, "The Anas," in *The Writings
of Thomas Jefferson. V.1.*, p. 278, https://babel.hathitrust.org/cgi/
pt?id=hvd.32044010456762&view=1up&seq=341&skin=2021

37. Paul Bentalou to Jefferson, August 9, 1786, https://founders.archi
ves.gov/documents/Jefferson/01-10-02-0136; Jefferson to Paul
Bentalou, August 25, 1786, https://founders.archives.gov/docume
nts/Jefferson/01-10-02-0216

38. Agreement with James Hemings, September 15, 1793, https://found
ers.archives.gov/documents/Jefferson/01-27-02-0127. See Annette
Gordon-Reed, *The Hemingses of Monticello: An American Family*
(New York: W.W. Norton, 2008).

39. Deed of Manumission for James Hemings, February 5, 1796, https://
founders.archives.gov/documents/Jefferson/01-28-02-0468

40. Francis Say to Jefferson, February 23, 1801, https://founders.archi
ves.gov/documents/Jefferson/01-33-02-0051

41. Jefferson to William Temple Franklin, July 16, 1790, https://found
ers.archives.gov/documents/Jefferson/01-17-02-0021; Jefferson to
William Temple Franklin, July 25, 1790, https://founders.archi
ves.gov/documents/Jefferson/01-17-02-0043; Jefferson to Mary

Jefferson, December 7, 1790, https://founders.archives.gov/docume nts/Jefferson/01-18-02-0096

42. Shippen quoted in James Morton Smith, ed., *The Republic of Letters: The Correspondence between Thomas Jefferson and James Madison, 1776–1826* (New York: W.W. Norton, 1995), Vol. 2, p. 663.

43. Jefferson to Madison, September 20, 1790, https://founders.archives.gov/?q=%20Author%3A%22Jefferson%2C%20Thomas%22%20Re cipient%3A%22Madison%2C%20James%22&s=1111311111&r=128. Four months later, Jefferson was still trying to settle on a price with Madison. Jefferson to Madison, January 10, 1791, https://found ers.archives.gov/?q=%20Author%3A%22Jefferson%2C%20Tho mas%22%20Recipient%3A%22Madison%2C%20James%22&s=111 1311111&r=134

44. Jefferson to Madison, March 13, 1790, https://founders.archives.gov-/?q=%20Author%3A%22Jefferson%2C%20Thomas%22%20Recipi ent%3A%22Madison%2C%20James%22&s=1111311111&r=138

45. Madison to Jefferson, March 13, 1791, https://founders.archives.gov/?q=%20Author%3A%22Madison%2C%20James%22%20Recipi ent%3A%22Jefferson%2C%20Thomas%22&s=1111311111&r=196

46. Jefferson to John Adams, July 17, 1791, https://founders.archives.gov/documents/Adams/99-02-02-1254; Jefferson to Jonathan B. Smith, April 26, 1791, https://founders.archives.gov/documents/Jefferson/01-20-02-0076-0002

47. Edmund Burke, *Reflections on the Revolution in France and on the Proceedings in Certain Societies in London Relative to That Event* (New York: Oxford University Press, 1993), p. 58.

48. Thomas Paine, *Rights of Man Being an Answer to Mr. Burke's Attack on the French Revolution* (London: J. S. Jordan, 1791), p. 3, 7, 11

49. Jefferson to Madison, January 30, 1787, https://founders.archives.gov/documents/Jefferson/01-11-02-0095

50. Tobias Lear to George Washington, May 8, 1791, https://founders.archives.gov/documents/Washington/05-08-02-0130

51. Tobias Lear to George Washington, May 8, 1791, https://founders.archives.gov/documents/Washington/05-08-02-0130

52. Jefferson to George Washington, May 8, 1791, https://founders.archives.gov/documents/Washington/05-08-02-0130

53. Jefferson to Madison, May 9, 1791, https://founders.archives.gov/documents/Madison/01-14-02-0015

54. Madison to Jefferson, May 12, 1791, https://founders.archives.gov/documents/Madison/01-14-02-0018

NOTES 135

55. Madison to Jefferson, May 12, 1791, https://founders.archives.gov/documents/Madison/01-14-02-0018

56. John Adams to Henry Knox, June 19, 1791, https://founders.archives.gov/documents/Adams/99-02-02-1249; Abigail Adams to Martha Washington, June 25, 1791, https://founders.archives.gov/documents/Adams/04-09-02-0121

57. Publicola, "Observations on Paine's Rights of Man. In a Series of Letters" (Edinburgh: J. Dickson, 1792), pp. 6, 7.

58. Madison to Jefferson, July 13, 1791, https://founders.archives.gov/documents/Madison/01-14-02-0037; James Madison to Thomas Jefferson, July 10, 1791, https://founders.archives.gov/documents/Madison/01-14-02-0034

59. Madison to Jefferson, July 13, 1791, https://founders.archives.gov/documents/Jefferson/01-20-02-0076-0008; Edmund Randolph to George Washington, July 13, 1791, https://founders.archives.gov/documents/Washington/05-08-02-0233#GEWN-05-08-02-0233-fn-0002-ptr; Edmund Randolph to Madison, July 21, 1791, https://founders.archives.gov/documents/Madison/01-14-02-0041

60. Jefferson to John Adams, July 17, 1791, https://founders.archives.gov/documents/Adams/99-02-02-1254

61. John Adams to Jefferson, July 29, 1791, https://founders.archives.gov/documents/Adams/99-02-02-1255

62. Jefferson to John Adams, August 30, 1791, https://founders.archives.gov/documents/Adams/99-02-02-1263

63. Jefferson to John Taylor, June 4, 1798, https://founders.archives.gov/documents/Jefferson/01-30-02-0280

64. Jefferson to Thomas Mann Randolph, Jr., May 15, 1791, https://founders.archives.gov/documents/Jefferson/01-20-02-0159

65. Jefferson to Thomas Mann Randolph, Jr., May 15, 1791, https://founders.archives.gov/documents/Jefferson/01-20-02-0159

66. Jefferson to Madison, July 21, 1791, https://founders.archives.gov/documents/Madison/01-14-02-0040

67. Jefferson to Philip Freneau, February 28, 1791, https://founders.archives.gov/documents/Jefferson/01-19-02-0087; Madison to Jefferson, May 1, 1791, https://founders.archives.gov/documents/Madison/01-14-02-0014; Jefferson to Madison, May 9, 1791, https://founders.archives.gov/documents/Madison/01-14-02-0015

68. Jefferson to Thomas Leiper, May 10, 1791, https://founders.archives.gov/?q=%20Author%3A%22Jefferson%2C%20Thomas%22%20Recipient%3A%22Leiper%2C%20Thomas%22&s=1111311111&r=3; Jefferson to Leiper, May 19, 1791, https://founders.archives.

136 NOTES

gov/?q=%20Author%3A%22Jefferson%2C%20Thomas%22%20Re
cipient%3A%22Leiper%2C%20Thomas%22&s=1111311111&r=4
69. Jefferson to Washington, May 15, 1791, https://founders.archi
ves.gov/?q=%20sugar%20Author%3A%22Jefferson%2C%20
Thomas%22%20Recipient%3A%22Washington%2C%20Geo
rge%22&s=1111311111&r=6
70. Alexander White to Mary Wood, March 8, 1789, https://rotunda.
upress.virginia.edu/founders/default.xqy?keys=FFCP-chron-1780
-1789-03-08-5&mode=deref; Madison to Ambrose Madison, May
19, 1791, https://founders.archives.gov/?q=%20Author%3A%-
22Madison%2C%20James%22%20Recipient%3A%22Madi
son%2C%20Ambrose%22&s=1111311111&r=21
71. Jefferson to Madison, July 21, 1791, https://founders.archives.gov/
documents/Madison/01-14-02-0040; Philip Freneau to James
Madison, July 25, 1791, https://founders.archives.gov/documents/
Madison/01-14-02-0047
72. Jefferson to Francis Hopkinson, March 13, 1789, https://found
ers.archives.gov/documents/Jefferson/01-14-02-0402; Madison
to Mann Page, Jr., [post 23] August 1791, https://founders.archi
ves.gov/documents/Madison/01-14-02-0066; "The Union Who
Are Its Real Friends," *National Gazette*, March 31, 1792, https://
founders.archives.gov/documents/Madison/01-14-02-0245. Also
see "Parties," *National Gazette*, ca. January 23, 1792, https://found
ers.archives.gov/documents/Madison/01-14-02-0176; Notes of
a Conversation with George Washington, May 23, 1793, https://
founders.archives.gov/documents/Jefferson/01-26-02-0092
73. George Washington to Jefferson, August 23, 1792, https://founders.
archives.gov/documents/Washington/05-11-02-0009
74. Jefferson to George Washington, September 9, 1792, https://found
ers.archives.gov/documents/Washington/05-11-02-0049
75. Jefferson to George Washington, September 9, 1792, https://found
ers.archives.gov/documents/Washington/05-11-02-0049
76. George Washington to Jefferson, October 18, 1792, https://found
ers.archives.gov/documents/Washington/05-11-02-0126
77. Franklin Bowditch Dexter, ed., *The Literary Diary of Ezra Stiles*
(New Yok: Charles Scribner's, 1901), Vol. III, p. 524; T. L. No.
I [July 25, 1792], https://founders.archives.gov/documents/Hamil
ton/01-12-02-0086

NOTES 137

78. Robert Troup to Alexander Hamilton, June 15, 1791, https://
founders.archives.gov/?q=%20Author%3A%22Troup%2C%20Rob
ert%22&s=1111311111&r=22&sr=

79. Temple quoted in "Editorial Note: The Northern Journey of
Jefferson and Madison," https://founders.archives.gov/documents/
Jefferson/01-20-02-0173-0001#TSJN-01-20-dg-0006-fn-0002-ptr;
Beckwith quoted in Frank T. Reuter, "'Petty Spy' or Effective
Diplomat: The Role of George Beckwith," *Journal of the Early
Republic* 10 (1990), p. 490.

80. The journey has not received much attention from scholars and is
usually addressed, if at all, in a few summary paragraphs in biog-
raphies of Jefferson and Madison. The most extensive discussion is
an editorial note in Julian P. Boyd, ed., "The Northern Journey of
Jefferson and Madison," *The Papers of Thomas Jefferson* (Princeton,
NJ: Princeton University Press, 1982), Vol. 20, pp. 434–453. Also see
Philip M. Marsh, "The Jefferson-Madison Vacation," *Pennsylvania
Magazine of History and Biography* 71 (January 1947), pp. 70–72; J.
Robert Maguire, ed., *The Tour of the Northern Lakes of James Madison
& Thomas Jefferson, May–June 1791* (Ticonderoga: Fort Ticonderoga,
1991); Willard Sterne Randall, "Thomas Jefferson Takes a Vacation,"
American Heritage (July–August 1996), pp. 74–85.

AT POUGHKEEPSIE: THE HESSIAN FLY (MAY 23)

1. The earliest reference to Madison being accompanied by a servant named Matthew is in Irving Brant, *James Madison: Father of
the Constitution, 1787–1800* (Indianapolis: Bobbs Merrill, 1950),
p. 338. Others have followed: Sydney N. Stokes, Jr., "A Visit to
Vermont," *Historic Roots* 4 (August 1999), p. 8; Nicholas Westbrook,
"Prince Taylor," in Henry Louis Gates and Evelyn Higginbotham,
eds., *African American National Biography* (New York: Oxford
University Press, 2008), pp. 516–517; and Noah Feldman, *The Three
Lives of James Madison* (New York: Random House, 2017), p. 329.
Adding to the mystery, Jefferson recorded in his memorandum
book paying Matthew 4.75 dollars at the end of the trip. Jefferson,
"Memorandum Books," 1791, https://founders.archives.gov/doc-
uments/Jefferson/02-02-02-0001#d1e21575a1048964-ptr. Ralph
Ketcham mentions two servants, but he does not name Matthew.
Ralph Ketcham, *James Madison: A Biography* (New York: Macmillan,
1971), p. 323; Jefferson to Madison, August 16, 1791, https://found

138   NOTES

ers.archives.gov/documents/Madison/01-17-02-0372; *Philadelphia General Advertiser*, January 7, 1791.

2. Jefferson to Madame de Tott, April 5, 1787, https://founders. archives.gov/?q=%20Author%3A%22Jefferson%2C%20Thomas%22%20Recipient%3A%22Tott%2C%20Sophie%20Ernestine%2C%20MMe%20de%22&s=1111311111&r=3

3. Washington to John Adams, May 10, 1789, https://founders.archives.gov/documents/Washington/05-02-02-0182; Donald Jackson and Dorothy Twohig, eds., *The Diaries of George Washington* (Charlottesville: University of Virginia Press, 1979), Vol. V, pp. 493, 472, 461, 470. On the tour, see T. H. Breen, *George Washington's Journey: The President Forges a Nation* (New York: Simon & Schuster, 2016).

4. Comments on Jefferson quoted in Lucia K. Stanton, "Hessian Fly," *Thomas Jefferson Encyclopedia*, https://www.monticello.org/site/research-and-collections/hessian-fly

5. Jefferson to Henry Remson, April 14, 1792, https://founders.archives.gov/documents/Jefferson/01-23-02-0377

6. Morgan quoted in Philip J. Pauly, "Fighting the Hessian Fly: American and British Responses to Insect Invasion," *Environmental History* 7 (July 2002), p. 488. Also see Brooke Hunter, "Creative Destruction: The Forgotten Legacy of the Hessian Fly," in Cathy Matson, ed., *The Economy of Early America: Historical Perspectives and New Directions* (University Park: Penn State University Press, 2006), pp. 236–262.

7. George Morgan to John Temple, August 26, 1788, in the Thomas Jefferson Papers, Library of Congress, https://www.loc.gov/item/mtjbib003757/

8. *The Prophet Nathan, or Plain Friend* (Hudson: Ashbel Stoddard, 1788), p. 10; William Hay to Thomas Jefferson, April 26, 1787, https://founders.archives.gov/documents/Jefferson/01-11-02-0303

9. Hay to Jefferson; Madison to Jefferson, July 24, 1788, https://founders.archives.gov/documents/Madison/01-11-02-0138; George Washington to George Morgan, August 25, 1788, https://founders.archives.gov/documents/Washington/04-06-02-0427; Richard Peters to George Washington, June 27, 1788, https://founders.archives.gov/documents/Washington/04-06-02-0320

10. George Washington to John Beale Bordley, August 17, 1788, https://founders.archives.gov/documents/Washington/04-06-02-0410; Madison to Jefferson, June 19, 1786, https://founders.archives.

NOTES   139

gov/documents/Madison/01-09-02-0017; Jefferson to George
Washington, May 10, 1789, https://founders.archives.gov/docume
nts/Jefferson/01-15-02-0115

11. See W. A., Low, "The Farmer in Post-Revolutionary Virginia,
1783–1789," *Agricultural History* 25 (1951), pp. 122–127 and Robert D.
Mitchell, "Agricultural Change and the American Revolution: A
Virginia Case Study," *Agricultural History* 47 (1973), pp. 119–132.

12. "Notes on the State of Virginia," in Merrill D. Peterson, ed., *The
Portable Thomas Jefferson* (New York: Penguin, 1975), p. 219; William
Hay to Thomas Jefferson, April 26, 1787, https://founders.archives.
gov/documents/Jefferson/01-11-02-0303

13. "On the Hessian Fly," *American Museum* 1 (February 1787), p. 133.

14. "Letter to Dr. Matty, on the effects of elder in preserving growing plants from insects and flies," *American Museum* 1 (February
1787), pp. 133–135; "Extract of a Letter from a Jersey Farmer, dated
Hunterdon, January 30, 1787," *American Museum* 1 (April 1787),
pp. 291–293.

15. "Letter on the Hessian Fly; addressed to the Society for Promoting
Agriculture," *American Museum* 1 (June 1787), pp. 456–459.

16. "Letter relative to the Hessian fly from col. Morgan, to the president
of the Philadelphia society for promoting agriculture," *American
Museum* 2 (September 1787), pp. 298–300.

17. George Morgan in "Proceedings of His Majesty's Most Honourable
Privy Council, and Information Received Respecting An Insect
Supposed to Infest the Wheat of the Territories of the United
States of America," in Arthur Young, ed., *Annals of Agriculture
and Other Useful Arts* 11 (1789), p. 529; George Morgan to George
Washington, August 25, 1788, https://founders.archives.gov/doc-
uments/Washington/04-06-02-0427; George Washington to John
Beale Bordley, August 17, 1788, https://founders.archives.gov/
documents/Washington/04-06-02-0410; George Washington to
Samuel Powel, December 15, 1789, https://founders.archives.gov/
documents/Washington/05-04-02-0291; George Washington to
William Pearce, November 2, 1794, https://founders.archives.gov/
documents/Washington/05-17-02-0089

18. "Proceedings of His Majesty's Most Honourable Privy Council,
and Information Received Respecting an Insect Supposed to Infest
the Wheat of the Territories of the United States of America," in
Young, *Annals of Agriculture and Other Useful Arts* 11 (1789), pp. 408,

140 NOTES

409; Benjamin Vaughan to John Vaughan, May 6, 1789, Benjamin Vaughan Papers, American Philosophical Society, Series 1, Box 1.

19. Jefferson to John Brown Cutting, October 2, 1788, https://founders.archives.gov/documents/Jefferson/01-13-02-0529; John Brown Cutting to Jefferson, October 17, 1788, https://founders.archives.gov/documents/Jefferson/01-14-02-0017; Thomas Paine to Jefferson, December 16, 1788, https://founders.archives.gov/documents/Jefferson/01-14-02-0144; Duke of Grafton quoted in Philip J. Pauly, *Fruits and Plains: The Horticultural Transformation of America* (Cambridge, MA: Harvard University Press, 2007), p. 46; Thomas Paine to Jefferson, February 16, 1789, https://founders.archives.gov/documents/Jefferson/01-14-02-0322

20. Samuel Powel to George Washington, September 9, 1788, https://founders.archives.gov/documents/Washington/04-06-02-0449; Thomas Jefferson to Benjamin Vaughan, May 17, 1789, https://founders.archives.gov/documents/Jefferson/01-15-02-0133

21. Jefferson to Benjamin Vaughan, May 17, 1789, https://founders.archives.gov/documents/Jefferson/01-15-02-0133

22. Wheat statistics quoted in "Proceedings of His Majesty's Most Honourable Privy Council," p. 420; Jefferson to Abigail Adams, June 21, 1785, https://founders.archives.gov/documents/Adams/04-06-02-0062

23. John W. Francis, *Reminiscences of Samuel Latham Mitchill* (New York: John Trow, 1859).

24. Samuel L. Mitchill, "An Account of the Insect; Which for Some Years Has Been Very Destructive to Wheat in Several of the United States," *American Magazine* (February and March 1788), pp. 173–176, 201–204. Also see Mitchill, "Short Memoir on the Wheat-Insect," June 23, 1791, Thomas Jefferson Papers, Library of Congress, https://www.loc.gov/resource/mtj1.014_0674_0677/

25. Mitchill, "An Account of the Insect," pp. 174–175; James Mease to Thomas Jefferson, October 12, 1792, https://founders.archives.gov/documents/Jefferson/01-24-02-0435; James Worth "On the Hessian Fly," *American Farmer* 3 (1822), p. 187. Also see "Memoir of the Hessian Fly," *American Farmer* 20 (1825), pp. 153–155.

26. Timothy Dwight, *Travels in New England and New York* (New Haven, CT: Timothy Dwight, 1822), Vol. III, pp. 300–301; *The Prophet Nathan*, pp. 4, 25.

27. American Philosophical Society Minutes, April 15, 1791, https://diglib.amphilsoc.org/islandora/object/american-philosophical-soci

NOTES 141

ety-minutes-1787-1793#page/1/mode/1up; Jefferson to Thomas
Mann Randolph, Jr., May 1, 1791, https://founders.archives.gov/
documents/Jefferson/01-20-02-0099

28. Jefferson to Benjamin S. Barton and others, May 12, 1791, https://
founders.archives.gov/documents/Jefferson/01-20-02-0138

29. Jefferson, "Notes on the Hessian Fly [May 24–June 18, 1791]," https://
founders.archives.gov/documents/Jefferson/01-20-02-0173-0003

30. *Albany Register* quoted in *New York Daily Advertiser*, June 6, 1791. See
discussion in "Editorial Note: The Northern Journey of Jefferson
and Madison," https://founders.archives.gov/documents/Jeffer
son/01-20-02-0173-0001#TSJN-01-20-dg-0006-fn-0007, note 7.

31. *Burlington Advertiser*, June 21, 1791, quoted in https://founders.archi
ves.gov/documents/Jefferson/01-20-02-0173-0001#TSJN-01-20-
dg-0006-fn-0008

32. Jefferson to Angelica Schuyler Church, August 17, 1788, https://
founders.archives.gov/documents/Jefferson/01-13-02-0400

33. Marquis de Chastellux, *Travels in North America, in the Years 1780–
81–82* (New York: NP, 1828), p. 174; Jefferson to Thomas Mann
Randolph, Jr., June 5, 1791, https://founders.archives.gov/docume
nts/Jefferson/01-20-02-0173-0007

34. Jefferson's Journal of the Tour, May 27, https://founders.archives.gov/
documents/Jefferson/01-20-02-0173-0002; Rayford W. Logan, ed.,
Memoirs of a Monticello Slave (Charlottesville: University of Virginia,
1951), pp. 28, 35; Jefferson to Henry Remsen, October 30, 1794,
https://founders.archives.gov/documents/Jefferson/01-28-02-0132

35. "Notes on the Hessian Fly"; Jefferson to Madison, June 21, 1791,
https://founders.archives.gov/?q=%22hessian%20fly%22&s=111
1311111&sa=&r=38&sr=

36. Jonathan Havens and Sylvester Dering to Jefferson, November 1, 1791,
https://founders.archives.gov/documents/Jefferson/01-22-02-0239;
Ezra L'Hommedieu to Jefferson, September 10, 1791, https://found
ers.archives.gov/documents/Jefferson/01-22-02-0136

37. Jefferson, "Notes on the Hessian Fly," [June 1–15, 1792], https://
founders.archives.gov/documents/Jefferson/01-24-02-0004

38. Jefferson to Thomas Mann Randolph, Jr., June 15, 1792, https://
founders.archives.gov/documents/Jefferson/01-24-02-0076

39. Hunter, "Creative Destruction," p. 253. Also see Brooke Hunter,
"Wheat, War, and the American Economy during the Age of
Revolution," *William and Mary Quarterly*, 3rd series, 62 (July 2005),

142 NOTES

pp. 505–526; Benjamin Henry LaTrobe, *The Journal of LaTrobe* (New York: D. Appleton, 1905), pp. 59–60

40. Charles Caldwell, *A Semi-Annual Oration, on the Origin of Pestilential Diseases* (Philadelphia: Bradfords, 1790), p. 30.

41. Jefferson to Thomas Mann Randolph, November 16, 1801, https://founders.archives.gov/documents/Jefferson/01-35-02-0517; Jefferson to James Monroe, May 5, 1811, https://founders.archives.gov/documents/Jefferson/03-03-02-0479; Jefferson to Madison, May 13, 1813, https://founders.archives.gov/documents/Jefferson/03-06-02-0122; Jefferson to William Johnson, May 10, 1817, https://founders.archives.gov/documents/Jefferson/03-11-02-0286

42. Madison to Jefferson, October 1, 1800, https://founders.archives.gov/?q=%22hessian%20fly%22&s=1111311111&sa=&r=81&sr=; Madison to Jefferson, July 8, 1811, https://founders.archives.gov/documents/Madison/03-03-02-0436; Madison to David Gelston, September 11, 1824, https://founders.archives.gov/?q=%22hessian%20fly%22&s=1111311111&sa=&r=160&sr=

AT FORT GEORGE: PRINCE TAYLOR (JUNE 1)

1. Jefferson to Martha Jefferson Randolph, May 31, 1791, https://founders.archives.gov/documents/Jefferson/01-20-02-0173-0006

2. Jefferson, Journal of the Tour, entry for May 29, https://founders.archives.gov/documents/Jefferson/01-20-02-0173-0002; Jefferson to Peter Carr, August 19, 1785, https://founders.archives.gov/documents/Jefferson/01-08-02-0319; Jefferson to Thomas Mann Randolph, Jr., June 5, 1791, https://founders.archives.gov/documents/Jefferson/01-20-02-0173-0007

3. Madison, Notes on the Lake Country Tour, entry for June 1, https://founders.archives.gov/documents/Jefferson/01-20-02-0173-0006; Jefferson, Journal of the Tour, entry for May 29, https://founders.archives.gov/documents/Jefferson/01-20-02-0173-0002

4. Eliot A. Cohen, *Conquered into Liberty: Two Centuries of Battles along the Great Warpath That Made the American Way of War* (New York: Simon & Schuster, 2011), p. 71; John F. Ross, *War on the Run: The Epic Story of Robert Rogers and the Conquest of America's First Frontier* (New York: Bantam, 2009), p. 165.

5. John Adams to Jefferson, July 10, 1787, https://founders.archives.gov/documents/Adams/06-19-02-0080; Abigail Adams to Jefferson, July 6, 1787, https://founders.archives.gov/documents/Jefferson

NOTES   143

son/01-11-02-0467; Abigail Adams to John Adams, September 22, 1774, https://www.masshist.org/digitaladams/archive/doc?id=L177 40922aa

6. Abigail Adams to Jefferson, July 6, 1787, https://founders.archives. gov/documents/Jefferson/01-11-02-0467

7. Jefferson to Mary Jefferson, May 30, 1791, https://founders.archives. gov/documents/Jefferson/01-20-02-0173-0005; Jefferson to Mary Jefferson, April 11, 1790, https://founders.archives.gov/documents/ Jefferson/01-16-02-0197

8. Letters of May 2, 1790, https://founders.archives.gov/documents/ Jefferson/01-16-02-0231; May 23, 1790, https://founders.archives. gov/documents/Jefferson/01-16-02-0255; July 4, 1790, https://found ers.archives.gov/documents/Jefferson/01-16-02-0255; July 25, 1790, https://founders.archives.gov/documents/Jefferson/01-17-02-0046; January 5, 1791, https://founders.archives.gov/documents/Jeffer son/01-18-02-0150

9. Mary Jefferson to Jefferson, April 25, 1790, https://founders.archi ves.gov/documents/Jefferson/01-16-02-0217; February 13, 1791, https://founders.archives.gov/documents/Jefferson/01-19-02-0046; March 26, 1791, https://founders.archives.gov/documents/Jeffer son/01-19-02-0169

10. Jefferson to Mary Jefferson, April 24, 1791, https://founders.archi ves.gov/documents/Jefferson/01-20-02-0067; May 8, 1791, https:// founders.archives.gov/documents/Jefferson/01-20-02-0121

11. Jefferson, Instructions for Meriweather Lewis, June 20, 1803, https:// founders.archives.gov/documents/Jefferson/01-40-02-0136-0005; Jefferson to Mary Jefferson, May 30, 1791, https://founders.archives. gov/documents/Jefferson/01-20-02-0173-0005

12. Jefferson to Mary Jefferson, May 30, 1791, https://founders.archives. gov/documents/Jefferson/01-20-02-0173-0005

13. Martha Jefferson Randolph to Jefferson, March 22, 1791, https:// founders.archives.gov/documents/Jefferson/01-19-02-0160

14. Jefferson to Martha Jefferson Randolph, December 23, 1790, https:// founders.archives.gov/documents/Jefferson/01-18-02-0127

15. Jefferson to Martha Jefferson Randolph, May 31, 1791, https:// founders.archives.gov/documents/Jefferson/01-20-02-0173-0006

16. Jefferson, Journal of the Tour, entry for May 29, https://founders. archives.gov/documents/Jefferson/01-20-02-0173-0002

17. Jefferson to Madison, March 16, 1784, https://founders.archives. gov/documents/Jefferson/01-07-02-0032

144 NOTES

18. Jefferson to Martha Jefferson Randolph, May 31, 1791, https://founders.archives.gov/documents/Jefferson/01-20-02-0173-0006
19. Madison, Notes on the Lake Country Tour, entry for May 31, https://founders.archives.gov/documents/Jefferson/01-20-02-0173-0006;
20. Madison, Notes on the Lake Country Tour, entry for June 1, https://founders.archives.gov/documents/Jefferson/01-20-02-0173-0006. Annette Gordon-Reed discusses the entry in *The Hemingses of Monticello* (New York: W.W. Norton, 2008), pp. 466–467.
21. The account of Taylor's life in this paragraph and the next draws heavily on Nicholas Westbrook, "Prince Taylor," in Henry Louis Gates and Evelyn Higginbotham, eds., *African American National Biography* (New York: Oxford University Press, 2008), pp. 516–517; Madison to Joseph Jones, November 28, 1780, https://founders.archives.gov/documents/Madison/01-02-02-0120
22. Elkanah Watson quoted in J. Robert Maguire, ed., *The Tour to the Northern Lakes of James Madison & Thomas Jefferson, May–June 1791* (Ticonderoga, NY: Fort Ticonderoga, 1995), pp. 10–11; Revolutionary War Pension and Bounty Land Warrant for Prince Taylor, Massachusetts, File S. 42,463, National Archives, https://catalog.archives.gov/id/196738230
23. Madison to Ambrose Madison, December 15, 1785, https://founders.archives.gov/documents/Madison/01-08-02-0231; Madison to Edmund Randolph, July 26, 1785, https://founders.archives.gov/?q=%20Author%3A%22Madison%2C%20James%22%20Recipient%3A%22Randolph%2C%20Edmund%22&s=1111311111&r=98; Madison to the editor of the Farmers' Register, March 22, 1836, https://founders.archives.gov/?q=worsted%20Author%3A%22Madison%2C%20James%22&s=1111311111&r=93&sr=; Jefferson to Jean Nicolas Demeunier, June 26, 1786, https://founders.archives.gov/documents/Jefferson/01-10-02-0001-0006
24. Gaillard Hunt, "William Thornton and Negro Colonization," *Proceedings of the American Antiquarian Society* 30 (April 1920), p. 48.
25. Madison, Memorandum on an African Colony for Freed Slaves, [ca. October 20] 1789, https://founders.archives.gov/documents/Madison/01-12-02-0287; Madison to Edward Coles, September 3, 1819, https://founders.archives.gov/documents/Madison/04-01-02-0456
26. Memorandum on an African Colony.
27. Hunt, "William Thornton and Negro Colonization," p. 52; Madison to Robert J. Evans, June 15, 1819, https://founders.archives.gov/documents/Madison/04-01-02-0421

NOTES   145

28. Madison to James Madison, Sr., September 8, 1783, https://found
ers.archives.gov/documents/Madison/01-07-02-0170

29. Petition for Freedom to the Massachusetts Council and House of
Representatives, January 1777, https://www.masshist.org/database/
viewer.php?item_id=557; James A. Bear, Jr. and Lucia C. Stanton,
eds., *Jefferson's Memorandum Books* (Princeton, NJ: Princeton
University Press, 1997), Vol. II, p. 808.

30. Jefferson to James Monroe, November 24, 1801, https://found
ers.archives.gov/documents/Jefferson/01-35-02-0550; Jefferson
to Rufus King, July 13, 1892, https://founders.archives.gov/doc-
uments/Jefferson/01-38-02-0052; Jefferson to Edward Coles,
August 25, 1814, https://founders.archives.gov/documents/Jeffer
son/03-07-02-0439

31. Merrill D. Peterson, ed., *The Portable Thomas Jefferson*
(New York: Penguin, 1977), pp. 186–189.

32. Benjamin Banneker to Jefferson, August 19, 1791, https://founders.
archives.gov/documents/Jefferson/01-22-02-0049

33. Jefferson to Benjamin Banneker, August 30, 1791, https://found
ers.archives.gov/documents/Jefferson/01-22-02-009; Jefferson to
Condorcet, August 30, 1791, https://founders.archives.gov/docume
nts/Jefferson/01-22-02-0092

34. Jefferson to Joel Barlow, October 8, 1809, https://founders.archi
ves.gov/documents/Jefferson/03-01-02-0461#D64046ID6. Also see
Jefferson to Henri Gregoire, February 25, 1809, https://founders.
archives.gov/?q=gregoire&s=1111311111&sa=&r=39&sr=

35. Edward Coles to Jefferson, July 31, 1814, https://founders.archives.
gov/documents/Jefferson/03-07-02-0374

36. Jefferson to Edward Coles, August 25, 1814, https://founders.archi
ves.gov/documents/Jefferson/03-07-02-0439; Edward Coles to
Jefferson, September 26, 1814, https://founders.archives.gov/doc-
uments/Jefferson/03-07-02-0494

37. Robert Pleasants to Madison, June 6, 1791, https://founders.archi
ves.gov/documents/Madison/01-14-02-0024

38. Madison to Robert Pleasants, October 30, 1791, https://founders.
archives.gov/documents/Madison/01-14-02-0086

39. Edward Coles to Madison, January 8, 1832, https://founders.archives.
gov/?q=Correspondent%3A%22Coles%2C%20Edward%22%20Co
rrespondent%3A%22Madison%2C%20James%22&s=1111311
111&r=56. In his will, Madison only left instructions that the
enslaved not be sold without consent so as to keep families intact.

146   NOTES

Dolley Madison ignored this provision. James Madison, "Original Will and Codicil of April 19, 1835," https://rotunda.upress.virginia.edu/founders/default.xqy?keys=FOEA-print-02-02-02-3114

40. Madison to Robert J. Evans, June 15, 1819, https://founders.archives.gov/documents/Madison/04-01-02-0421; Madison to Lafayette, October 7, 1821, https://founders.archives.gov/documents/Madison/04-02-02-0336

AT BENNINGTON: SUGAR MAPLE (JUNE 4–5)

1. James Madison, "Notes on the Lake Country Tour," June 2, https://founders.archives.gov/documents/Madison/01-14-02-0023; Thomas Jefferson, Journal of the Tour, June 3, https://founders.archives.gov/documents/Madison/01-14-02-0023

2. Madison, "Notes," June 3 and 4.

3. Madison, "On the Settlement of Disputes between States by Judicial Means, after June 1784," https://founders.archives.gov/?q=vermont%20Author%3A%22Jefferson%2C%20Thomas%22&s=1111311111&r=6&sr=

4. Jefferson to Edmund Randolph, February 15, 1783, https://founders.archives.gov/documents/Jefferson/01-06-02-0228

5. Ethan Allen quoted in "Editorial Note: The Admission of Kentucky and Vermont to the Union," https://founders.archives.gov/documents/Jefferson/01-19-02-0103-0001

6. Washington and memorial quoted in "Editorial Note: The Admission of Kentucky and Vermont to the Union," https://founders.archives.gov/documents/Jefferson/01-19-02-0103-0001; Journal of the Senate, February 7, 1791.

7. Nathaniel Chipman to Alexander Hamilton, July 14, 1788, https://founders.archives.gov/?q=Chipman%20to%20Hamilton%2C%2014%20July%201788%20&s=1111311111&sa=&r=1&sr=; Hamilton to Chipman, July 22, 1788, ers.archives.gov/?q=Chipman to Hamilton%2C 14 July 1788 &s=1111311111&sa=&r=3&sr=

8. *Vermont Gazette*, June 6, 1791.

9. *Vermont Gazette*, June 13, 1791.

10. Joseph Fay to Jefferson, September 20, 1791, https://founders.archives.gov/?q=joseph%20fay%20Author%3A%22Fay%2C%20Joseph%22&s=1111311111&r=2&sr=

11. Jefferson to Washington, June 5, 1791, https://founders.archives.gov/documents/Jefferson/01-20-02-0173-0008; Jefferson to

NOTES 147

Thomas Chittenden, July 9, 1792, https://founders.archives.gov-/?q=%20chittenden%20Recipient%3A%22Chittenden%2C%20Thomas%22&s=1111311111&r=4

12. Jefferson to Washington, June 5, 1791, https://founders.archives.gov/documents/Jefferson/01-20-02-0173-0008

13. Jefferson to Thomas Mann Randolph, June 5, 1791, https://founders.archives.gov/documents/Jefferson/01-20-02-0173-0007; Jefferson to Washington, June 5, 1791, https://founders.archives.gov/documents/Jefferson/01-20-02-0173-0008

14. Philip Schuyler to John Schuyler, May 26, 1791, quoted in "Editorial Note: The Northern Journey of Jefferson and Madison," https://founders.archives.gov/documents/Jefferson/01-20-02-0173-0001

15. Chase quoted in Kevin J. Weddle, *The Compleat Victory: Saratoga and the American Revolution* (New York: Oxford University Press, 2021), p. 376; David Ramsay, *The History of the American Revolution* (Philadelphia: R. Aitken and Son, 1789), II, p. 55.

16. Duc de la Rochefoucault Liancourt, *Travels through the United States of North America* (London: T. Gilbert, 1800), Vol. II, p. 65; William L. Stone, *Visits to the Saratoga Battle Ground, 1780–1880* (Albany, NY: Joel Munsell's Sons, 1895), p. 165.

17. Weddle, *Compleat Victory*, p. 246; Washington to Israel Putnam, August 22, 1777, https://founders.archives.gov/?q=putnam%20Recipient%3A%22Putnam%2C%20Israel%22&s=1111311111&r=68

18. Jefferson to John Stark, August 19, 1805, https://founders.archives.gov/?q=stark&s=1111311111&r=25&sr=stark%2C%20john; Madison to John Stark, December 26, 1809, https://founders.archives.gov/?q=stark&s=1111311111&r=26&sr=stark%2C%20john; John Stark to James Madison, January 21, 1810, https://founders.archives.gov/?q=stark%20Author%3A%22Stark%2C%20John%22&s=1111311111&r=38&sr=

19. George Washington to Philip John Schuyler, July 15, 1783, https://founders.archives.gov/documents/Washington/99-01-02-11597

20. Timothy Dwight, *The Nature and Danger of Infidel Philosophy* (New Haven: George Bunce, 1798); William Sprague, *Annals of the American Pulpit* (New York: Robert Carter, 1866), Vol. I, p. 643.

21. Jefferson to Ezra Stiles, July 25, 1819, https://founders.archives.gov/documents/Jefferson/03-14-02-0428

22. Moses Robinson to Jefferson, March 3, 1801, https://founders.archives.gov/documents/Jefferson/01-33-02-0112; Jefferson to Robinson, March 23, 1801, https://founders.archives.gov/docume

148

NOTES

nts/Jefferson/01-33-02-0362; New England Palladium quoted in Frederick C. Luebke, "The Origins of Thomas Jefferson's Anti-Clericalism," p. 349, https://digitalcommons.unl.edu/cgi/viewcont ent.cgi?article=1180&context=historyfacpub

23. Jefferson to Robinson, March 23, 1801, https://founders.archives. gov/documents/Jefferson/01-33-02-0362

24. Jefferson to Thomas Mann Randolph, June 5, 1791, https://found ers.archives.gov/documents/Jefferson/01-20-02-0173-0007

25. Jefferson to Thomas Cooper, October 7, 1814, https://founders. archives.gov/documents/Jefferson/03-08-02-0007; Jefferson to Madame de Tesse, March 27, 1811, https://founders.archives.gov- /?q=tesse&s=1111311111&sa=&r=161&sr=; Jefferson to Bernard McMahon, February 16, 1812, https://founders.archives.gov- /?q=mcmahon&s=1111311111&sa=&r=83&sr=. See Andrea Wulf, *Founding Gardeners: The Revolutionary Generation, Nature and the Shaping of the American Nation* (New York: Vintage, 2011).

26. Madison, "Notes on the Lake Country Tour," June 6, https:// founders.archives.gov/documents/Madison/01-14-02-0023. For a good overview, see Mary B. Donchez, "A Sweet Legacy? Thomas Jefferson and the Development of the Maple Sugar Industry in Vermont" (master's thesis, Harvard University, 2017), https:// dash.harvard.edu/bitstream/handle/1/37736749/DONCHEZ-DOCUMENT-2017.pdf?sequence=1&isAllowed=y

27. Robert Beverly, *The History and Present State of Virginia in Four Parts* (London: R. Parker, 1705), Part II, p. 21.

28. Richard Saunders, *Poor Richard Improved* (Philadelphia: B. Franklin, 1765), https://founders.archives.gov/?q=%22sugar%20ma ple%22&s=1111311111&sa=&r=2&sr=#BNFN-01-12-02-00 01-fn-0012-ptr

29. "Advantages of the Culture of the Sugar Maple Tree," in *American Museum: or Repository* (Philadelphia: Matthew Carey, 1788), Vol. 4, p. 350; George W. Corner, ed., *The Autobiography of Benjamin Rush* (Westport, CT: Greenwood, 1970), p. 177. Also see *Remarks on the Manufacturing of Maple Sugar* (Philadelphia: James and Johnson, 1790).

30. J. P. Brissot de Warville, *New Travels in the United States in the United States of America Performed in 1788* (Dublin: W. Corbet, 1792), p. 301.

31. *The Journal of John Woolman* (Boston: Houghton Mifflin, 1871), p. 231

32. *An Address to the People of Great Britain on the Utility of Refraining from the Use of West India Sugar and Rum* (Sunderland: T. Reed, 1791), p. 4. The most common version of the title substituted

NOTES 149

propriety for utility. On the campaign, see Julie L. Holcomb, *Moral Commerce: Quakers and the Transatlantic Boycott of the Slave Economy* (Ithaca, NY: Cornell University Press, 2020).

33. Henry Biddle, ed., *Extracts from the Journal of Elizabeth Drinker, from 1759 to 1807* (Philadelphia: Lippincott, 1889), p. 222.

34. Tench Coxe, *A View of the United States of America* (Philadelphia: William Hall, 1794), pp. 77–82; Warville, *New Travels*, pp. 303–304.

35. Corner, *Autobiography of Benjamin Rush*, p. 181; Jefferson to Benjamin Vaughan, June 27, 1790, https://founders.archives.gov-/?q=%22sugar%20maple%22%20Author%3A%22Jefferson%2C%20Thomas%22&s=1111311111&r=3&sr=; Madison, *Notes for Speech in Congress* [ca. May 13, 1790], https://founders.archives.gov-/?q=maple%20Author%3A%22Madison%2C%20James%22&s=111 1311111&r=7&sr=

36. Jefferson to Thomas Mann Randolph, May 1, 1791, https://found ers.archives.gov/?q=%22sugar%20maple%22%20Author%3A%22Je fferson%2C%20Thomas%22&s=1111311111&r=8&sr=; Jefferson to George Washington, May 1, 1791, https://founders.archives.gov-/?q=%22sugar%20maple%22%20Author%3A%22Jefferson%2C%20Thomas%22&s=1111311111&r=6&sr=#GEWN-05-08-02-01 10-fn-0004-ptr;

37. Drinker quoted in David W. Maxey, "The Union Farm: Henry Drinker's Experiment in Deriving Profit from Virtue," *Pennsylvania Magazine of History and Biography* 107 (October 1983), p. 618; Jefferson, Journal of the Tour, June 5, 1791; Jefferson to Thomas Mann Randolph, June 4, 1791, https://founders.archives.gov/documents/Jefferson/01-20-02-0173-0007; *Vermont Gazette*, June 13, 1791.

38. Seth Jenkins to Jefferson, July 5, 1791, https://founders.archives.gov/documents/Jefferson/01-20-02-0251; Beckwith quoted in "Editorial Note: The Northern Journey of Jefferson and Madison," https://founders.archives.gov/documents/Jefferson/01-20-02-0173-0001

39. Madison to Jefferson, December 9, 1787, https://founders.archives.gov/?q=Correspondent%3A%22Madison%2C%20James%22%20Co rrespondent%3A%22Jefferson%2C%20Thomas%22%20Da tes-To%3A1791-01-01&s=1111311111&r=223

40. George Washington Diaries, October 10, 1789, https://founders.archives.gov/?q=set%20off%20from%20New%20York%2C%20ab out%20on ine%200%E2%80%99clock%20in%20my%20ba rge%2C%20to%20visit%20Mr.%20Prince%E2%80%99s%20fr

150 NOTES

uit%20gardens%20and%20shrubberies%20at%20Flushing&s=111
1311111&sa=&r=1&sr; Jefferson to William Prince, July 6,
1791, https://founders.archives.gov/?q=%22william%20pri
nce%22&s=11113111111&sa=&r=14&sr=

41. Jefferson to Thomas Mann Randolph, December 1790, https://found
ers.archives.gov/?q=%22sugar%20maple%22%20Author%3A%22Je
fferson%2C%20Thomas%22&s=11113111111&r=4&sr=; Thomas
Jefferson to Nicholas Lewis, July 29, 1787, https://founders.archi
ves.gov/?q=grasses%20Author%3A%22Jefferson%2C%20Tho
mas%22&s=11113111111&r=22&sr=

42. Thomas Mann Randolph to Jefferson, July 7, 1791, https://
founders.archives.gov/?q=%22sugar%20maple%22&s=1111311
111&sa=&r=26&sr=; Jefferson to Thomas Mann Randolph, April
19, 1792, https://founders.archives.gov/?q=%22sugar%20ma
ple%22%20Author%3A%22Jefferson%2C%20Thomas%22&s=111
1311111&r=15&sr=

43. Jefferson to Hugh Rose, July 2, 1791, https://founders.archives.gov-
/?q=%22sugar%20maple%22%20Author%3A%22Jefferson%2C%20
Thomas%22&s=11113111111&r=12&sr=; Jefferson to Madison,
July 6, 1791, https://founders.archives.gov/?q=%22william%20
prince%22&s=11113111111&sa=&r=13&sr=#JSMN-01-14-02-00
33-fn-0001-ptr; Madison to Jefferson, July 10, 1791, https://found
ers.archives.gov/documents/Madison/01-14-02-0034

44. Jefferson to Joseph Fay, August 30, 1791, https://founders.
archives.gov/?q=Correspondent%3A%22Jefferson%2C%20Tho
mas%22%20Correspondent%3A%22Fay%2C%20Joseph%22&s=111
1311111&r=2; Joseph Fay to Thomas Jefferson, November 29, 1791.

45. Jefferson to William Short, November 25, 1791, https://founders.
archives.gov/documents/Jefferson/01-22-02-0305

46. Arthur Noble and William Cooper quoted in Thomas Jefferson
to George Washington, May 1, 1791, editorial note, https://found
ers.archives.gov/documents/Jefferson/01-20-02-0101; George
Washington to Anthony Whitting, November 4, 1792, https://
founders.archives.gov/documents/Washington/05-11-02-0182

47. Benjamin Rush, *An Account of the Sugar-Maple Tree of the United
States* (Philadelphia: R. Aitken, 1792), p. 12.

48. Rush, *An Account*, p. 11.

49. On Cooper's involvement with maple sugar, see Alan Taylor,
*William Cooper's Town: Power and Persuasion on the Frontier of the Early
American Republic* (New York: Vintage, 1996).

NOTES 151

50. Alexander Hamilton to William Cooper, August 3, 1791, https://founders.archives.gov/documents/Hamilton/01-09-02-0006; John Lincklaen, *Travels in the Years 1791 and 1792 in Pennsylvania, New York, and Vermont* (New York: G.P. Putnam's, 1897), p. 85, 88.

51. See Khalil Gibran Muhammed, "The Sugar That Saturates the American Diet Has a Barbaric History as the 'White Gold' that Fueled Slavery," *New York Times*, August 14, 2019, https://www.nytimes.com/interactive/2019/08/14/magazine/sugar-slave-trade-slavery.html

52. Jefferson to C. P. de Lasteyrie, July 15, 1808, https://founders.archives.gov/?q=%22sugar%20maple%22%20Author%3A%22Jefferson%2C%20Thomas%22&s=1111311111&r=21&sr=; Thomas Jefferson to Thomas Lomax, November 6, 1809, https://founders.archives.gov/?q=%22sugar%20maple%22%20Author%3A%22Jefferson%2C%20Thomas%22&s=1111311111&r=22&sr=

AT POOSPATUCK: UNKECHAUG INDIANS (JUNE 14)

1. "Notes on the Lake Country Tour," entry for June 6, https://founders.archives.gov/documents/Madison/01-14-02-0023.

2. "Notes on the Lake Country Tour," entry for June 7, https://founders.archives.gov/documents/Madison/01-14-02-0023

3. Jefferson to Madison, June 21, 1791, https://founders.archives.gov-/?q=%20Author%3A%22Jefferson%2C%20Thomas%22%20Recipient%3A%22Madison%2C%20James%22&s=1111311111&r=142

4. Nathaniel Hazard to Alexander Hamilton, November 25, 1791, https://founders.archives.gov/?q=%20Author%3A%22Hazard%2C%20Nathaniel%22&s=1111311111&r=7&sr=

5. John C. Hamilton, *History of the Republic of the United States* (New York: D. Appleton, 1859), 4:506.

6. Franklin Bowditch Dexter, ed., *The Literary Diary of Ezra Stiles* (New Yok: Charles Scribner's, 1901), Vol. III, p. 125.

7. Jefferson to David Humphreys, March 18, 1789, https://founders.archives.gov/documents/Jefferson/01-14-02-0422

8. Jefferson's Journal of the Tour, entry for June 3, https://founders.archives.gov/documents/Jefferson/01-20-02-0173-0002; Jefferson to Benjamin Vaughan, June 27, 1790, https://founders.archives.gov/documents/Jefferson/01-16-02-0342

9. Jefferson to Madison, April 14, 1783, https://founders.archives.gov/?q=%20Author%3A%22Jefferson%2C%20Thomas%22%20Re

152 NOTES

cipient%3A%22Madison%2C%20James%22&s=111131111&r=18; Madison to Jefferson, April 22, 1783, https://founders.archives. gov/?q=%20Author%3A%22Madison%2C%20James%22%20Recipi ent%3A%22Jefferson%2C%20Thomas%22&s=111131111&r=46

10. Madison to Jefferson, August 11, 1783, https://founders.archives. gov/?q=%20Author%3A%22Madison%2C%20James%22%20Recipi ent%3A%22Jefferson%2C%20Thomas%22&s=111131111&r=58

11. See John A. Strong, *The Unkechaug Indians of Eastern Long Island* (Norman: University of Oklahoma Press, 2011), and Jennifer Anderson, "'A Laudable Spirit of Enterprise': Renegotiating Land, Natural Resources, and Power on Post-Revolutionary Long Island," *Early American Studies: An Interdisciplinary Journal* 13 (Spring 2015), pp. 413–442.

12. Jefferson, "A Bill for Amending the Constitution of the College of William and Mary," https://founders.archives.gov/documents/ Jefferson/01-02-02-0132-0004-0080

13. Jefferson to John Adams, June 11, 1812, https://founders.archi ves.gov/documents/Jefferson/03-05-02-0100; Jefferson to Constantin Volney, December 17, 1796, https://founders.archi ves.gov/documents/Jefferson/01-29-02-0183; Jefferson to Marquis Chastellux, June 7, 1785, https://founders.archives.gov/docume nts/Jefferson/01-08-02-0145; Jefferson, speech to Jean Baptiste DuCoigne, June 1, 1781, https://founders.archives.gov/docume nts/Jefferson/01-06-02-0059. See Anthony F. C. Wallace, *Jefferson and the Indians: The Tragic Fate of the First Americans* (Cambridge. MA: Harvard University Press, 1999).

14. Jefferson to William Phillips, July 22, 1779, https://founders.archi ves.gov/documents/Jefferson/01-03-02-0052; Jefferson to George Rogers Clark, January 1, 1780, https://founders.archives.gov/doc-uments/Jefferson/01-03-02-0289

15. Jefferson to Henrick Aupumut, December 21, 1808, https://found ers.archives.gov/documents/Jefferson/99-01-02-9358. Also see Jefferson to Benjamin Hawkins, February 18, 1803, https://found ers.archives.gov/documents/Jefferson/01-39-02-0456. See Bernard Sheehan, *Seeds of Extinction: Jeffersonian Philanthropy and the American Indian* (Chapel Hill: University of North Carolina, 1973).

16. Count de Buffon, *Natural History: General and Particular* (London: A. Strahan, 1791), Vol. 5, p. 136. See Lee Alan Dugatkin, *Mr. Jefferson and*

NOTES 153

the Giant Moose: Natural History in Early America (Chicago: University of Chicago Press, 2009).

17. Jefferson, *Notes on the State of Virginia* (Philadelphia: Prichard and Hall, 1788), https://docsouth.unc.edu/southlit/jefferson/jeffer son.html

18. Madison to Jefferson, June 19, 1786, https://founders.archives.gov/ documents/Madison/01-09-02-0017

19. Jefferson, *Notes on the State of Virginia*, p. 46.

20. Jefferson, *Notes on the State of Virginia*, p. 61; p. 63; pp. 99–100.

21. Jefferson, *Notes on the State of Virginia*, p. 107.

22. Jefferson to Ezra Stiles, September 1, 1786, https://founders.archi ves.gov/documents/Jefferson/01-10-02-0233; Jefferson to Benjamin Hawkins, August 13, 1786, https://founders.archives.gov/docume nts/Jefferson/01-10-02-0159, and August 4, 1787, https://founders. archives.gov/documents/Jefferson/01-11-02-0591. On Jefferson's vocabulary project, see Wallace, *Jefferson and the Indians* and Sarah Rivett, "Unruly Empiricisms and Linguistic Sovereignty in Thomas Jefferson's Indian Vocabulary Project," *American Literature* 87 (December 2015), pp. 645–680.

23. Benjamin Hawkins to Jefferson, June 14, 1786, https://founders. archives.gov/documents/Jefferson/01-09-02-0536#TSJN-01-0 9-0539-kw-0001; Jefferson to Madison, January 12, 1789, https:// founders.archives.gov/documents/Jefferson/01-14-02-0208

24. Marquis de Lafayette to George Washington, February 10, 1786, https://founders.archives.gov/documents/Washing ton/04-03-02-0469; George Washington to Lafayette, May 10, 1786, https://founders.archives.gov/documents/Washing ton/04-04-02-0051; Richard Butler to George Washington, November 30, 1787, https://founders.archives.gov/documents/Was hington/04-05-02-0419-0001; Madison to George Washington, March 18, 1787, https://founders.archives.gov/documents/Madi son/01-09-02-0168; George Washington to Marquis de Lafayette, January 10, 1788, https://founders.archives.gov/documents/Was hington/04-06-02-0023

25. See Rivett, "Unruly Empiricisms." Jefferson to Benjamin Smith Barton, September 21, 1809, https://founders.archives.gov/docume nts/Jefferson/03-01-02-0430

26. Jefferson to David Campbell, March 14, 1800, https://founders. archives.gov/documents/Jefferson/01-31-02-0375

154 NOTES

27. Jefferson to George Washington, June 5, 1791, https://founders.archives.gov/documents/Jefferson/01-20-02-0173-0008; Jefferson to James Monroe, July 10, 1791, https://founders.archives.gov/documents/Jefferson/01-20-02-0076-0007; Jefferson to Martha Jefferson Randolph, June 23, 1791, https://founders.archives.gov/documents/Jefferson/01-20-02-0217

28. Madison to Jefferson, July 10, 1791, https://founders.archives.gov/documents/Jefferson/01-20-02-0266; James Madison to James Madison, Sr., July 2, 1791, https://founders.archives.gov/?q=%20Author%3A%22Madison%2C%20James%22%20Recipient%3A%22Madison%2C%20James%2C%20Sr.%22&s=1111311111&r=61

29. "Vocabulary of the Delaware Indians," American Indian Vocabulary Collection, American Philosophical Society, https://diglib.amphilsoc.org/islandora/object/17-vocabulary-delaware-indians

30. William Vans Murray to Jefferson, September 18, 1792, https://founders.archives.gov/documents/Jefferson/01-24-02-0360; Jefferson to William Linn, February 5, 1798, https://founders.archives.gov/?q=Author%3A%22Jefferson%2C%20Thomas%22%20Recipient%3A%22Linn%2C%20William%22&s=1111311111&r=2; Jefferson to William Dunbar, June 24, 1799, https://founders.archives.gov/documents/Jefferson/01-31-02-0120; Jefferson to David Campbell, March 14, 1800, https://founders.archives.gov/documents/Jefferson/01-31-02-0375

31. Jefferson to John Sibley, May 27, 1805, https://founders.archives.gov/?q=%20Author%3A%22Jefferson%2C%20Thomas%22%20Recipient%3A%22Sibley%2C%20John%22&s=1111311111&r=1

32. Jefferson to William Dunbar, January 12, 1801, https://founders.archives.gov/documents/Jefferson/01-32-02-0322; Jefferson to David Campbell, March 14, 1800, https://founders.archives.gov/?q=%20Author%3A%22Jefferson%2C%20Thomas%22%20Recipient%3A%22Campbell%2C%20David%22&s=1111311111&r=3; Jefferson to Benjamin Hawkins, March 14, 1800, https://founders.archives.gov/?q=Author%3A%22Jefferson%2C%20Thomas%22%20Recipient%3A%22Hawkins%2C%20Benjamin%22&s=1111311111&r=6

33. Jefferson to David Campbell, March 14, 1800, https://founders.archives.gov/?q=%20Author%3A%22Jefferson%2C%20Thomas%22%20Recipient%3A%22Campbell%2C%20David%22&s=1111311111&r=3

NOTES

155

34. Jefferson to William Dunbar, January 12, 1801, https://founders. archives.gov/documents/Jefferson/01-32-02-0322; Jefferson to John Pickering, February 13, 1822, https://founders.archives.gov-/?q=%20Author%3A%22Jefferson%2C%20Thomas%22%20Recipient%3A%22Pickering%2C%20John%22&s=1111311111&r=2

35. "Jefferson's Instructions for Meriweather Lewis," https://www.loc. gov/exhibits/lewisandclark/transcript57.html

36. Jefferson to Jose Correa da Serra, April 26, 1816, http://www.let. rug.nl/usa/presidents/thomas-jefferson/letters-of-thomas-jefferson/jefl244.php. See Bob Saindon, "The Indian Vocabularies," https://lewis-clark.org/sciences/ethnography/indian-vocabularies/.

37. Jefferson to Levett Harris, April 18, 1806, https://founders.archives. gov/documents/Jefferson/99-01-02-3593

38. Jefferson to Benjamin Smith Barton, September 21, 1809, https:// founders.archives.gov/?q=Author%3A%22Jefferson%2C%20Thomas%22%20Recipient%3A%22Barton%2C%20Benjamin%20Smith%22&s=1111311111&r=27; George Jefferson to Jefferson, June 26, 1809, https://founders.archives.gov/?q=%20Author%3A%22Jefferson%2C%20George%22%20Recipient%3A%22Jefferson%2C%20Thomas%22&s=1111311111&r=263.

39. Jefferson to Benjamin Smith Barton, September 21, 1809, https:// founders.archives.gov/?q=%20Author%3A%22Jefferson%2C%20Thomas%22%20Recipient%3A%22Barton%2C%20Benjamin%20Smith%22&s=1111311111&r=27

40. Benjamin Smith Barton to Jefferson, October 18, 1810, https://founders.archives.gov/documents/Jefferson/03-03-02-0107; Jefferson to Peter S. Du Ponceau, December 30, 1817,

41. Peter S. Du Ponceau to Jefferson, July 12, 1820, https://founders. archives.gov/?q=%20Recipient%3A%22Jefferson%2C%20Thomas%22&s=1111311111&sa=du%20ponceau&r=15; Jefferson to Peter Wilson, January 20, 1816, https://founders.archives.gov/documents/Jefferson/03-09-02-0242; Jefferson to John Pickering, February 20, 1825, https://founders.archives.gov/?q=Author%3A%22Jefferson%2C%20Thomas%22%20Recipient%3A%22Pickering%2C%20John%22&s=1111311111&r=4

42. Jefferson to Constantine Samuel Rafinesque, August 11, 1824, https://founders.archives.gov/documents/Jefferson/98-01-02-4452

43. Patricia Cohen, "Indian Tribes Go in Search of Their Lost Languages," *New York Times*, August 6, 2010, https://www.nytimes. com/2010/04/06/books/06language.html

156 NOTES

EPILOGUE: FAREWELLS

1. Linda J. Docherty, "Gilbert Stuart's Companion Portraits of Thomas Jefferson and James Madison," *American Art* 22 (Summer 2008), p. 93; James Madison to Robley Dunglison, October 14, 1831, https://founders.archives.gov/documents/Madison/99-02-02-2459

2. Jefferson to Angelica Schuyler Church, November 27, 1793, https://founders.archives.gov/documents/Jefferson/01-27-02-0416; Jefferson to Madison, April 27, 1795, https://founders.archives.gov/documents/Jefferson/01-28-02-0258; Jefferson to Madison, April 3, 1794, https://founders.archives.gov/documents/Madison/01-15-02-0197

3. Dolley Madison quoted in James Morton Smith, ed., *The Republic of Letters* (New York: W.W. Norton, 1995), II, 847; Jefferson to Madison, December 28, 1794, https://founders.archives.gov/documents/Jefferson/01-28-02-0171; Madison to Jefferson, March 23, 1795, https://founders.archives.gov/documents/Jefferson/01-28-02-0230; John Adams to Abigail Adams, January 14, 1797, https://founders.archives.gov/?q=%20Author%3A%22Adams%2C%20John%22%20Recipient%3A%22Adams%2C%20Abigail%22&s=1111311111&r=621

4. Jefferson to Littleton W. Tazewell, January 5, 1805, https://founders.archives.gov/?q=%20Author%3A%22Jefferson%2C%20Thomas%22%20Recipient%3A%22Tazewell%2C%20Littleton%20W.%22&s=1111311111&r=6

5. Jefferson to Madison, April 15, 1817, https://founders.archives.gov/?q=%20Author%3A%22Jefferson%2C%20Thomas%22%20Recipient%3A%22Madison%2C%20James%22%20Period%3A%22post-Madison%20Presidency%22&s=1111311111&r=6

6. Jefferson to the Trustees of the Lottery for East Tennessee College, May 6, 1810, https://founders.archives.gov/documents/Jefferson/03-02-02-0322. For a brief account see "Jefferson's Plan for an Academical Village," Thomas Jefferson, Monticello, https://www.monticello.org/research-education/thomas-jefferson-encyclopedia/jeffersons-plan-academical-village/#fn-5. The best full history is Alan Taylor, *Thomas Jefferson's Education* (New York: W.W. Norton, 2019).

7. Margaret Bayard Smith, *Forty Years of Washington Society* (New York: Scribner, 1906), p. 235.

8. Margaret H. Smith, August 20, 1830, https://founders.archives.gov/?q=%22little%20journal%22&s=1111311111&sa=&r=3&sr=

NOTES

157

9. James Madison to Margaret Bayard Smith, September 21, 1830, https://founders.archives.gov/documents/Madison/99-02-02-2160

10. Ellen Wayles Randolph Coolidge to Jefferson, August 1, 1825, https://founders.archives.gov/?q=Correspondent%3A%22Je fferson%2C%20Thomas%22%20Correspondent%3A%22Cooli dge%2C%20Ellen%20Wayles%20Randolph%22&s=1111311 111&r=66

11. Jefferson to Ellen Wayles Randolph Coolidge, August 27, 1825, https://founders.archives.gov/documents/Jefferson/98-01-02-5493.

12. Jefferson to William Short, September 8, 1823, https://founders.archi ves.gov/documents/Jefferson/98-01-02-3750; Thomas Jefferson, *Notes on the State of Virginia* (Philadelphia: Prichard and Hall, 1788), p. 173; Jefferson to John Holmes, April 22, 1820, https://found ers.archives.gov/?q=%20Author%3A%22Jefferson%2C%20Tho mas%22&s=1111311111&r=2&sr=holmes%2C%20john; Jefferson's Autobiography, https://avalon.law.yale.edu/19th_century/jeffa uto.asp.

13. Jefferson to Ellen Wayles Randolph Coolidge, August 27, 1825, https://founders.archives.gov/documents/Jefferson/98-01-02-5493.

14. Jefferson to William Gordon, January 1, 1826, https://found ers.archives.gov/?q=%20Author%3A%22Jefferson%2C%20 Thomas%22%20Recipient%3A%22Gordon%2C%20Will iam%22&s=1111311111&r=5; Jefferson to Madison, February 17, 1826, https://founders.archives.gov/?q=%20Author%3A%22Jeffer son%2C%20Thomas%22%20Recipient%3A%22Madison%2C%20Ja mes%22&s=1111311111&r=1183

15. Jefferson to Madison, February 17, 1826, https://founders.archives. gov/?q=%20Author%3A%22Jefferson%2C%20Thomas%22%20Re cipient%3A%22Madison%2C%20James%22&s=1111311111&r=1183. See Annette Gordon-Reed, "'Take Care of Me When Dead': Jefferson Legacies," *Journal of the Early Republic* 40 (Spring 2020), pp. 1–17.

16. Madison to Jefferson, February 24, 1826, https://founders.archives. gov/documents/Madison/04-03-02-0714

17. Madison to Henry D. Gilpin, October 25, 1827, https://found ers.archives.gov/?q=%20Author%3A%22Madison%2C%20Ja mes%22&s=1111311111&r=3&sr=gilpin

18. Thomas Jefferson: Will and Codicil, March 16–17, 1826, March 16, 1826, https://founders.archives.gov/documents/Jeffer son/98-01-02-5963

19. Madison to Thomas Jefferson Randolph, July 14, 1826, https://founders.archives.gov/?q=%20Author%3A%22Madison%2C%20James%22&s=1111311111&r=164&sr=randolph

Further Reading

There are several dual biographies of Jefferson and Madison, including Lance Banning, *Jefferson & Madison: Three Conversations from the Founding* (New York: Rowman & Littlefield, 1995), Jeff Broadwater, *Jefferson, Madison, and the Making of the Constitution* (Chapel Hill: University of North Carolina Press, 2019), Andrew Burstein and Nancy Isenberg, *Madison and Jefferson* (New York: Random House, 2013), Adrienne Koch, *Jefferson and Madison: The Great Collaboration* (New York: Oxford University Press, 1964), and Andrew Shankman, *Original Intents: Hamilton, Jefferson, Madison and the American Founding* (New York: Oxford University Press, 2017).

Individual biographies of each abound. On Jefferson, see John B. Boles, *Jefferson: Architect of American Liberty* (New York: Basic Books, 2017), Nobel E. Cunningham, Jr., *In Pursuit of Reason: The Life of Thomas Jefferson* (Baton Rouge: Louisiana State University Press, 1987), Joseph J. Ellis, *American Sphinx: The Character of Thomas Jefferson* (New York: Vintage, 1998), John Ferling, *Jefferson and Hamilton: The Rivalry That Forged a Nation* (New York: Bloomsbury, 2013), Thomas Kidd, *Thomas Jefferson: A Biography of Spirit and Flesh* (New Haven, CT: Yale University Press, 2022), Dumas Malone, *Jefferson and His Time*, 6 vols. (New York: Little, Brown, 1948–1981), Jon Meacham, *Thomas Jefferson: The Art of Power* (New York: Random House, 2013), and Gordon Wood, *Friends Divided: John Adams and Thomas Jefferson* (New York: Penguin, 2017).

Biographies of Madison include Irving Brant, *James Madison: Father of the Constitution, 1787–1800* (Indianapolis: Bobbs-Merrill, 1941), Richard Brookhiser, *James Madison* (New York: Basic Books, 2011), Lynne Cheney, *James Madison: A Life Reconsidered* (New York: Viking, 2014), James Cost, *James Madison: America's First Politician* (New York: Basic Books, 2021), Noah Feldman, *The Three Lives of James Madison* (New York: Random House, 2017), Drew R. McCoy, *The Last of the Fathers: James Madison & the Republican Legacy* (New York: Cambridge University Press, 1991), Richard K. Matthews, *If Men Were Angels: James Madison and the Heartless Empire of Reason* (Lawrence: University of Kansas Press, 1995), Jack N. Rakove, *James Madison and the Creation of the American*

Republic (New York: Pearson, 2006), Jack N. Rakove, *A Politician Thinking: The Creative Mind of James Madison* (Norman: University of Oklahoma Press, 2017), Colleen A. Sheehan, *The Mind of James Madison* (Cambridge: Cambridge University Press, 2015), and Jack Signer, *Becoming Madison: The Extraordinary Origins of the Least Likely Founding Father* (New York: Public Affairs, 2015).

Jefferson's travels are the subject of Edward Dumbauld, *Thomas Jefferson: American Tourist* (Norman: University of Oklahoma Press, 1946), and George Green Shackleford, *Jefferson's Travels in Europe, 1784–1789* (Baltimore: Johns Hopkins University Press, 1995). On science and natural history, see Silvio Bedini, *Thomas Jefferson: Statesman of Science* (New York: Macmillan, 1990), Lee Alan Dugatkin, *Mr. Jefferson's Moose: Natural History in Early America* (Chicago: University of Chicago Press, 2009), and Andrea Wulf, *Founding Gardeners: The Revolutionary Generation, Nature, and the Shaping of the American Nation* (New York: Vintage, 2011).

On Jefferson and slavery, see Annette Gordon-Reed, *Thomas Jefferson & Sally Hemmings: An American Controversy* (Charlottesville: University of Virginia Press, 1998), Annette Gordon-Reed, *The Hemingses of Monticello: An American Family* (New York: Norton, 2009), and Lucia C. Stanton, *"Those Who Labor for My Happiness:" Slavery at Thomas Jefferson's Monticello* (Charlottesville: University of Virginia Press, 2012). On Native Americans, see Bernard Sheehan, *Seeds of Extinction: Jeffersonian Philanthropy and the American Indian* (Chapel Hill: University of North Carolina, 1973), and Anthony F. C. Wallace, *Jefferson and the Indians: The Tragic Fate of the First Americans* (Cambridge, MA: Harvard University Press, 1999).

Index

For the benefit of digital users, indexed terms that span two pages (e.g., 52–53) may, on occasion, appear on only one of those pages.

Figures are indicated by an italic *f* following the page number.

An Account of the Sugar Maple-Tree of the United States (Rush), 92–94
Adams, Abigail, 7, 27, 58–59
Adams, John
  Discourses on Davila and views on French Revolution of, 24–25, 26, 29
  Federalist views of centralized power and, 24–25
  Franklin and, 11
  international travel by, 1–2
  Jefferson and, 11, 24–25, 26–27, 28–29, 116–18
  Madison and, 11, 26–27
  political parties and, xi
  presidency of, 29
  Rights of Man (Paine) and, 25–26
Adams, John Quincy, xii, 27
Alburgh (Vermont), 78
Allen, Ethan, 75, 77
American Philosophical Society, 12, 113
American Revolution
  Bennington, battle (1777) of, 80–81
  free Black soldiers in, 64–66
  Hessian mercenaries in, 41
  Native Americans and, 100

Saratoga, Battle (1777) of, 79
Virginia and, 9
Anti-Federalists, 15, 95–96
Articles of Confederation, 13–14

Bache, Benjamin Franklin, 29
Banks, Joseph, 45–46, 48
Banneker, Benjamin, 70–71
Barbe-Mabois, Francois, 5, 101
Barton, Benjamin Smith, 48–49, 83–84, 112, 113
Beckley, John, 23–24, 26–27
Beckwith, George, 23, 25, 26–27, 33, 89
Bennington (Vermont), 74, 80–82, 95, 121–22
Bentalou, Paul, 20
Beverly, Robert, 84
Biddle, Nicholas, 113
"Billey" (William Gardner), 37, 68–69, 70
Bill of Rights (US Constitution), 15–16, 96
Bond, Phineas, 45–46
Bowdoin, James, 115
Brissot de Warville, J.P., 86
Brotherton (Delaware Indian reservation), 107

INDEX

Brown, Jabez, 97
Buffon, Comte Georges-Louis
    de, 100–2
Bull, Frederick, 96
Burgoyne, John, 79, 80
Burke, Edmund, 24
Burr, Aaron, 33, 50
Burwell, Rebecca, 1
Butler, Richard, 103–4
Butler, Weeden, 104–6

Campbell, David, 106, 107–8
Canada, 78–79
Carmarthen, Lord, 45–46
Catherine the Great (tsarina of
    Russia), 103–4
Chase, Samuel, 79
Chipman, Nathaniel, 75–77
Chittenden, Thomas, 76, 78
Clark, William, 111, 113
Coles, Edward, 67, 71–73
College of William and
    Mary, 99–100
*Comparative Vocabularies of Several
    Indian Languages* (Jefferson),
    108–11, 110*f*, 113
Condorcet, 71
Constitutional Convention
    (1787), 11, 13
Coolidge, Ellen Wayles
    Randolph, 120
Cooper, John, 38
Cooper, William, 87, 92, 93–94
Cosway, Maria, 13
Coxe, Tench, 87, 93–94
Cutting, John Brown, 46

Delaware Indians, 107
Democratic-Republicans, xi–xii,
    24–25, 50, 77–78, 97
Dewey, Elijah, 81–82
Discourses on Davila (John Adams),
    24–25, 26, 29
Drayton, William, 88

Drinker, Henry, 87, 88–89, 93–94
Dunbar, William, 107–8
Du Ponceau, Peter, 113–14
Dutchman's Point (Vermont), 78
Dwight, Timothy, 48, 82

East Springfield
    (Massachusetts), 95–96
Edwards, Jonathan, 104–6
Edwards, Pierpont, 96
Ellicott, Andrew, 71
*Essay on a Uniform Orthography for
    the Indian Languages of North
    America* (Pickering), 108–11

Fay, Joseph, 77–78, 91–92
Federalists
    Bill of Rights and, 15
    centralized power favored
        by, 24–25
    Jefferson's deist beliefs
        and, 81–83
    in New England, 96
    Paine and, 27–28
    travels of Jefferson and Madison
        to northern states (1791) and,
        33, 96–97
    in Vermont, 82–83
Fenno, John, 29, 32
Floyd, Catherine "Kitty," 11,
    12, 98–99
Floyd, Nicoll, 99
Floyd, William, 98–99
Fort Crown Point, 79
Fort Edward, 74, 79, 121–22
Fort George, 64, 79, 121–22
Fort Ticonderoga, 79, 81, 121–22
Fort William Henry, 79
Fox, Charles, 50
Fox, William, 86–87
Franklin, Benjamin
    Adams (John) and, 11
    American Philosophical Society
        and, 12

INDEX

163

international travel by, 1
slavery opposed by, 72
Stiles and, 97
sugar maple trees and, 84
Franklin, William Temple, 21–22
French Revolution, 24–25, 47
Freneau, Philip, 29–30, 31, 32, 33

Gardner, Henrietta, 68–69
Gardner, William ("Billey"), 37,
  68–69, 70
Gates, Horatio, 79
Gazette of the United States,
  29, 31, 32
General Advertiser newspaper
  (Philadelphia), 29
Granger, Sr., George, 91

Hamilton, Alexander
  Constitution of the United
    States and, 15
  Federalist views of centralized
    power and, 24–25
  international travel by, 1
  Jefferson and, 16, 18–19,
    26, 32, 97
  Madison and, 16, 18–19,
    26–27, 97
  maple sugar production and, 94
  national capital location
    and, 16, 19
  national debt debates and, 16–19
  political parties and, xi
  Vermont's land disputes with
    New York and, 76
  Washington and, 32–33, 81
Hamilton, John C., 97
Hancock, John, 97
Hartford (Connecticut), 96, 97
Haswell, Anthony, 77, 88–89
Hawkins, Benjamin, 103
Hay, William, 41
Hazard, Nathaniel, 96
Hemings, Elizabeth, 19–20

Hemings, James (slave of Thomas
  Jefferson), 7, 19–21, 37, 69, 97
Hemings, James Madison (son and
  slave of Thomas Jefferson), 70
Hemings, Peter, 21
Hemings, Sally, 58–59, 69, 70
Hessian fly
  American Museum coverage
    of, 44–45
  Jefferson's efforts regarding, 30,
    95, 98, 99, 106, 107
  Long Island and, 98, 99
  wheat crop damaged by, 30
Hessian mercenaries in the
  Revolutionary War, 41
Holland Land Company, 94
House, Mary, 11, 22
Huntington, Samuel, 96

Iroquois Indians, 5
Irving, Washington, 39

Jefferson, Maria "Polly," 58–61
Jefferson, Thomas. *See also* travels
  of Jefferson and Madison to
  northern states (1791)
  Adams (John) and, 11, 24–25,
    26–27, 28–29, 116–18
  as ambassador to France (1785-
    1789), 47
  American Philosophical Society
    and, 12, 113
  Banneker and, 70–71
  Bill for Establishing Religious
    Freedom (1786), 81–82
  botany as a passion of, 83–84
  Buffon and, 100–2
  chess and, 12–13
  children fathered into
    slavery by, 70
  Constitutional Convention
    (1787) and, 11
  Constitution of the United
    States and, 14–16

Jefferson, Thomas (*cont.*)
death of, 122–23
death of wife of, 10–11
deism and views of religion of,
81–82, 83
election of 1796 and, 116–18
Freneau and, 29–30, 31, 32
as governor of Virginia during
American Revolution, 9
Hamilton and, 16, 18–19,
26, 32, 97
health of, 7–8, 107, 115–16, 119
Hessian fly and, 30, 95, 98, 99,
106, 107
international travel by,
1–3
Lewis and Clark Expedition
and, 111
Madison's final meeting (1826)
with, 122
as Minister Plenipotentiary
to Paris peace negotiations
(1784-1789), 10–12, 19–20, 97
national capital location
and, 16, 19
national debt debates and, 16,
17, 18–19
Native Americans and, 14,
99–101, 102–3, 104–6, 105*f*,
107–14, 110*f*
Patent Act and, 98
Philadelphia residences of,
21–22, 23
political parties and, xi, 31
portrait by Stuart of, 115, 116*f*
Prince's Nursery and, 89, 91
real estate transactions in
Virginia and, 12, 13
republican newspaper supported
by, 29, 31, 32
retirement (1809) of, 118
Rights of Man (Paine) and, 23–29
as secretary of state, 16, 33, 47,
97–98, 115–16

Shays's Rebellion (1786-1787)
and, 14–15, 97
slavery and emancipation views
of, 66, 69, 71–72, 120–21
slaves owned by, 7, 19–21,
72–73, 91
sugar maple trees and maple
sugar promoted by, 84, 88–92,
94, 107
tariff policy and, 122–23
theft of Indian grammar research
(1809) of, 112–13
University of Virginia and,
118, 122
as vice president, 118
Virginia General Assembly
(1776) and, 8
walking stick of, 123*f*, 123–24
Washington and, 22–23,
25–26, 32–33
weather as a topic of interest
for, 62
white supremacy doctrine
supported by, 69–71, 121
will of, 123
Jenkins, Seth, 89
Johnson, William, 57, 58, 96

Kentucky, admission to the union
(1792) of, 76–77

Lafayette, Marquis de,
4–5, 103–4
Lake Champlain, 57, 62–64
Lake George, 57–58, 62, 81
Lasher, Conrad, 39, 49
Lay, Benjamin, 86
Lear, Tobias, 25–26
Leiper, Thomas, 21–22, 30
Lewis, Meriweather, 111, 112–13
Lincklaen, John, 94
Linn, William, 107–8
Livingston, Robert, 33
Logan, Chief, 102

INDEX

Long Island (New York), 98, 99, 121–22
Louisiana, 94
Louisiana Purchase, 111

Madison, Dolley Payne Todd, 72–73, 99, 116–18
Madison, James. *See also* travels of Jefferson and Madison to northern states (1791)
Adams (John) and, 11, 26–27
American Philosophical Society and, 12
Bill for Establishing Religious Freedom (1786), 81–82
Buffon and, 101
chess and, 12–13
Constitutional Convention (1787) and, 11, 13
Constitution of the United States and, 15–16
death of, 123–24
election of 1796 and, 116–18
Floyd's broken engagement with, 11, 12, 98–99
free Black soldiers in American Revolution and, 64–66
Freneau and, 29–30, 31
Hamilton and, 16, 18–19, 26–27, 97
health of, 3, 8, 91, 107, 119
invitation to France from Jefferson declined (1784) by, 3
Jefferson's final meeting (1826) with, 122
Jefferson's posthumous legacy and, 122–23
Jefferson's walking stick and, 123–24
Lafayette's travels to northern states (1784) with, 4–5
Monroe's invitation to travel with, 3–4

Montpelier estate of, 22–23
national capital location and, 16, 19
national debt debates and, 17–19
Native Americans and, 107
Philadelphia residence of, 22, 23
political parties and, xi, 31
portrait by Pine of, 115
portrait by Stuart of, 115, 117*f*
Prince's Nursery and, 89
real estate transactions in Virginia and, 12, 13
republican newspaper supported by, 29, 31
retirement (1817) of, 118
sea travel feared by, 98
Shays's Rebellion (1786-1787) and, 13–14, 97
slavery and emancipation views of, 66–68, 72–73
slaves owned by, 68–69, 72–73
sugar maple trees and maple sugar promoted by, 84, 88, 92
University of Virginia and, 118, 122
Virginia General Assembly (1776) and, 8
War of 1812 and, 118
Washington and, 22–23
Massachusetts
abolition of slavery (1783) in, 68–69, 120–21
ratification of the US Constitution (1788) in, 15–16, 95–96
Shays's Rebellion in, 98, 121–22
McMahon, Bernard, 83–84
Missouri crisis (1820), 121
Mitchill, Samuel Latham, 47–48, 54
Monroe, James
Madison invited to travel by, 3–4
real estate holdings of, 12, 13
University of Virginia and, 118

166 INDEX

Morgan, George, 39–41, 44–45
Morris, Lewis, 75–76
Morris, Robert, 76–77
Murray, William Vans, 107–8

Nanticoke Indians, 107–8
National Gazette newspaper, 31, 33
Native Americans
  American Revolution and, 100
  Buffon's views of, 100–1, 102
  Jefferson's views and studies of,
    14, 99–101, 102–3, 104–6,
    105*f*, 107–14, 110*f*
  Lafayette's visit (1784)
    with, 6
  languages of, 103–6, 105*f*,
    107–11, 110*f*, 113–14
  Lewis and Clark Expedition
    and, 111
  Madison's studies of, 107
  treaties and, 100
  Washington and, 100, 103–4
Noble, Arthur, 88, 92
Northampton (Massachusetts),
  13–14, 95–96
Notes on the State of Virginia
  (Jefferson), 43–44, 69–
  70, 101–3
Nottoway Indians, 113–14

Observations on Modern Gardening
  (Whately), 1–2
Osgood, Samuel, 27–28

Page, John, 1
Paine, Thomas, 27–28, 46. *See also*
  Rights of Man (Paine)
Pallas, Peter Simon, 104–6, 111
Payne, Anna, 12–13
Pennsylvania, abolition of slavery
  (1780) in, 20, 68
Philadelphia (Pennsylvania)
  Constitutional Convention
    (1787) in, 11, 13

French Revolution and, 25
Jefferson's residences in, 21–
  22, 23
Madison's residences in, 22, 23
newspapers during 1790s in, 29,
  31, 32, 33
as temporary national capital, 19
Pickering, John, 108–11
Pickering, Timothy, 27–28
Pine, Robert Edge, 115
Pleasants, Robert, 72
Point au Fer (New York), 78
Pomeroy's Red Tavern
  (Northampton, MA), 95–96
Poospatuck settlement, 99. *See also*
  Unkechaug Indians
Powel, Samuel, 46
Prince's Nursery (Flushing, New
  York), 89, 90*f*, 91, 106
Publicola essays, 27, 28–29

Ramsay, David, 79
Randolph, Anne Cary, 61
Randolph, Benjamin Franklin, 61
Randolph, Edmund, 25–26, 27–28
Randolph, James Madison, 61
Randolph, Martha Jefferson
  ("Patsy"), 58–59, 61–62, 97
Randolph, Thomas Mann (son-
  in-law of James Madison), 61,
  91, 123–24
Reflections on the Revolution in France
  (Burke), 24
Rights of Man (Paine), 23–26,
  27–29, 77–78
Rittenhouse, David, 26
Robinson, Moses, 77, 81–83
Rochefoucauld, Duc, 79–80
Rogers, Robert, 58
Rush, Benjamin, 86, 87, 88, 92–94
Rutledge, Jr., John, 2

Saint-Domingue slave revolt
  (1791), 91–92

INDEX

Saratoga (New York), 79–80, 81, 121–22
Schuyler, John, 79
Schuyler, Philip, 33, 79, 84, 120
Shays's Rebellion (1786-1787), 13–15, 97
Shippen, Thomas Lee, 2–3, 22
Short, William, 12, 13
Sibley, John, 108
Skelton, Martha Wayles, 10–11, 19–20
slavery
  colonization movement and, 66–68, 69, 73
  Franklin's opposition to, 72
  Jefferson's slaves and, 7, 19–21, 72–73, 91
  Jefferson's views of, 66, 69, 71–72, 120–21
  Madison's slaves and, 68–69, 72–73
  Madison's views of, 66–68, 72–73
  Massachusetts's abolition (1783) of, 68–69, 120–21
  Missouri crisis (1820) and, 121
  Pennsylvania's abolition (1780) of, 20, 71
  Saint-Domingue revolt (1791) and, 91–92
  sugar production and, 86–87, 93, 94
Smith, Jonathan Bayard, 23
Smith, Margaret Bayard, 119
Smith, Samuel Harrison, 23–24
Society for the Abolition of the Slave Trade, 86–87
Stark, John, 80–81
Stiles, Ezra, 33, 97
Stuart, Gilbert, 115, 116f, 117f
Sugar Act (1764), 84
sugar maple trees
  abolitionists' promotion of sugar made from, 86, 87, 93

cane sugar dependence reduced by, 84, 86, 88, 91–92, 93
  commercial setbacks for maple sugar production and, 93–94
  at Fort Edward, 74
  illustration of leaves of, 85f
  Jefferson's interest in, 84, 88–92, 94, 107
  Madison's interest in, 84, 88, 92
  Prince's Nursery and, 89, 91
  Rush's promotion of sugar produced from, 86, 88, 92–93
  in Vermont, 88–89, 94, 95
  Washington's interest in, 87, 92
Swift, Job, 82

Taylor, Prince, 64–66, 65f, 69, 70, 73
Temple, John, 33
Tesse, Madame de, 83–84
Thornton, William, 66–68
travels of Jefferson and Madison to northern states (1791)
  American Revolution battle sites and, 79–80
  birch bark as material for letter-writing on, 60–61
  dates of, xi
  distilleries and, 89
  end of, 107
  expenses on, 106
  Federalists and, 33, 96–97
  free Blacks in New York State and, 64–66
  Hartford (Connecticut) and, 96
  inns rated by Jefferson on, 40f
  Jefferson's later reflections on, 121–22
  Jefferson's preparations for, 7, 26, 30–31
  Lake George and, 57–58, 62, 81
  Long Island and, 98, 121–22
  Madison's later reflections on, 119–20

168 INDEX

travels of Jefferson and Madison to
northern states (1791) (*cont.*)
Madison's preparations
for, 7, 27
Unkechaug Indians and,
104, 106
Vermont and, 77–78, 80, 81–82,
83, 84, 88
weather during, 62–63
Treaty of Fort Finney
(1786), 4
Treaty of Fort Stanwix (1784), 5
Troup, Robert, 33
Trumbull, Jonathan, 96, 97

University of Virginia, 118, 122
Unkechaug Indians
efforts in twenty-first century to
revive language of, 114
Jefferson's study of Native
American languages and,
104–6, 105*f*, 113
Poospatuck settlement and, 99
travels of Jefferson and Madison
to lands (1791) of, 104, 106
whaling and, 104, 106

Vaughan, Benjamin, 45–46
Vermont
admission to the union (1791)
of, 76–77
botany of, 83
British military posts after
American Revolution in, 78
Democratic-Republican
politicians in, 77–78
emigrants from Massachusetts
and Connecticut in, 74
Federalists in, 82–83
New York's land disputes (1777-
1791) with, 75–76
ratification of US Constitution
(1791) by, 15–16, 76–77
Sabbath laws in, 81–82, 94

sugar maple trees in, 88–89, 94, 95
travels by Jefferson and Madison
(1791) in, 77–78, 80, 81–82,
83, 84, 88
Virginia
abolitionists in, 72
American Revolution and,
9, 17–18
Bill for Establishing Religious
Freedom (1786) and, 81–82
climate of, 62–63
General Assembly session
(1776) in, 8
Native Americans in, 102–3
ratification of the US
Constitution and, 15–16
University of Virginia and,
118, 122

Wallace, Harry, 114
War of 1812, 96, 118
Washington, George
Bennington, battle
(1777) of, 80
farming by, 43
free Black soldiers in American
Revolution and, 64–66
Hamilton and, 32–33
Hessian fly and, 41–43
international travel by, 1
Jefferson and, 22–23, 25–
26, 32–33
Lafayette and, 4
Madison and, 22–23
Native Americans and,
100, 103–4
New York State land
purchases by, 81
political parties and, 32
postmaster general and, 27–28
Prince's Nursery and, 89
Rights of Man (Paine) and,
24, 25–26
slaves owned by, 20

Stuart's portrait of, 115
sugar maple trees and maple
  sugar promoted by, 87, 92
travel to American Revolution
  battle sites (1783) by, 81
Vermont's admission to the

union (1791) and, 75–76
Washington, Martha, 25
Wayles, John, 19–20
Whately, Thomas, 1–2
Wolcott, Oliver, 96
Woolman, John, 86